Analyzing People's Behavior: Learn How to Speed Read a Human and Analyze Their Personality

Analyzing People's Behavior: Learn How to Speed Read a Human and Analyze Their Personality

introduction

The human mind helps you learn, make decisions, and know what someone else is saying. This is why you need to understand the various aspects of body language and how it relates to your life.

When you understand how your mind works, you will be able to live a more fulfilling life. And make better connections. Much has been done to demystify the human mind, but people don't always make use of information.

Armed with the right information, you can reach your goals faster than ever. You can also achieve more as a human being.

This book is for the person trying to make sense of how their mind works. It is also for the person trying to have a better understanding of their life, their relationships and anything in between.

Do you always find it difficult to turn people down, even if you don't want to do what they ask of you? It is a key skill for a person to learn how to reject people. There are many men, however, who suffer from this problem - people who start saying yes to every request they get, and so on; as a result, they end up getting involved in things they don't want to do. Well don't worry, there are real ways to say "no" to people without sounding like a complete idiot. Here are some tips on how to turn people down while keeping your manhood.

Resumes could be seen as a painting of a human being demonstrating himself by demonstrating his competence, career goals and work experience. When writing their own resume, very few people take advantage of it to use it. While this is essentially the purpose of a resume, you should be careful when creating your resume. From an objective perspective, you need to look at your resume. In other words, your resume shouldn't be biased but it should reflect the truth about you.

Manipulation isn't ethical, but we need to know how to subtly manipulate people and influence their decisions in this dog-eat-dog world. Now, I'm not saying you're going out on the street and manipulating everyone you meet. Use these strategies to your advantage. Sometimes you can also use these techniques to get positive results.

The power of influence, manipulation and seduction is now a subject that you can make sense of and with which you no longer need to feel alienated or broken. Understand what positive influence really means and how to use it alongside other deliberate practices for maximum results. You also learned what to watch out for in terms of the negative manipulation going on around you and focusing on you.

Additionally, you've completed the initial and crucial steps for reading others and influencing social, business, or romantic interactions. As you have developed these chapters, you have expanded your knowledge of the history of manipulation and how it plays a role in today's media as well. You are now more aware of the professionals who continually rely on these applications for their success. Hopefully, you have gained understanding, confidence and practical application from the information contained in this book.

Not only have you become familiar with the practices required to become an excellent reader of the body language and voice communications of others, but you have also learned that positive and deliberate persuasion can help you repair existing relationships that may be experiencing strain.

When your life seems out of your control, you can change direction with deliberate influence. When you get it wrong or forget what to do, the exercises in this book will get you back to the point and help you get back to the actual work once again. You are encouraged to continue practicing regularly with the wealth of knowledge you now have, to expand your knowledge and evolve once again.

Practical and ethical influence and manipulation will take you far. With this information in this book, you are ready to stop bowing to the will of others and start implementing the life and future you want with persuasion tactics.

Chapter 1 Introduction to the Psychology of Human Behavior

Human behavior, while we are all unique, follows relatively predictable trends. People tend to behave the same way in similar situations. Because of this, it becomes easy to analyze those behaviors and understand what is going on in someone else's mind. This is exactly what human behavior analysis strives to do: it wants to understand what is happening in another's mind and take control of the behaviors to influence it.

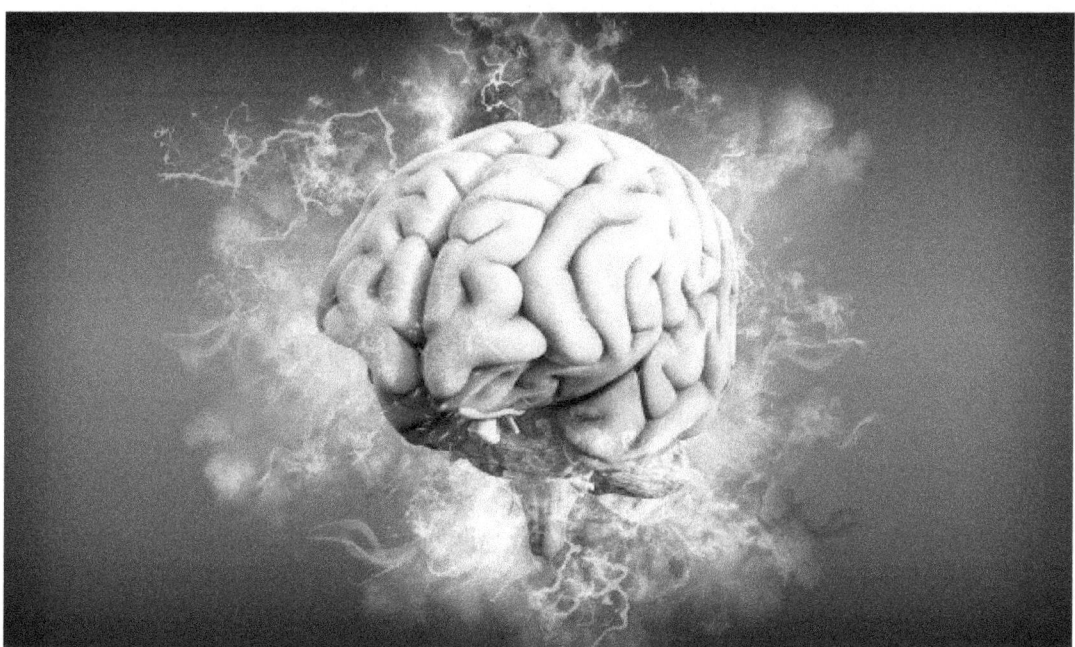

In its simplest form, behavior analysis refers to a science that understands the behaviors of other people. Study how biology affects behaviors and how behaviors can change based on context. If you take the time to learn another person's common patterns and behaviors, you are able to notice the patterns and understand the causes of each behavior, which allows you to focus on changing the behaviors by interrupting or redirecting them in some way.

There are several ways to control other people's behaviors, from appealing to authority to the way things are expressed. Regardless of how you choose how to control another person, it can be used in ways that influence the other person to act in certain ways simply because you are able to read and redirect their behaviors the right way. Here are some of the ways you can control an individual's behaviors. Identify the strengths

When you identify someone else's strengths, you set things up so you can recognize what they do well and can play with them later. For example, if you understand that someone is skilled enough in art, you may be able to redirect them to do something you want them to do because you know they are good at it.

Consciousness

Consciousness is seen as a behavioral state in which you are aware of yourself at that moment. You can control someone's behaviors by making them suddenly acutely aware of what they are doing at the moment, for example, and you can tell a child that they are actively doing something, which you can then make them stop. When you activate awareness of one thing, you may be able to influence another, such as drawing attention to fiddling with your hands, which may distract from another attempt to persuade or influence an individual.

Cold reading

Cold reading refers to the idea that people spread information vague enough for almost anyone to identify it, and make inferences by observing the other person's behavior. Think of a psychic pretending to read a crystal ball - he might say something vague about someone wanting to contact you on the other side, and you might complain that it must be your dear aunt Ellie who recently passed away. This gave her the information she needed to move forward and convince you that she was right. Cold reading in behavior analysis is similar: the individual says something and watches your reactions, essentially going on a fishing expedition.

Priming

Priming refers to the idea that one stimulus can create an influence on what will happen with the second stimulus. Think about the subliminal messages here: You are shown one thing you may have a good or bad thought about, and then shown a second thing. You can encourage people to associate a relatively neutral word, such as banana, with a completely foreign concept, such as friendly simply by repeatedly introducing friendly before or after the banana.

Linguistics

The way you use words is very important: you can use certain words and phrases in certain ways to encourage certain types of behavior. Using words with positive connotations are much more likely to trigger positive behaviors than negative words. Think of NLP with this concept: You can appeal to a person using words that are meaningful or relevant to that individual.

Confusion as a weapon

When confusion is used against you, you are much more likely to accept what you are asked to do. Because you are confused, your mind is worried, it tries to calculate what just happened and it becomes vulnerable to whatever the other person is trying to suggest. This is useful in manipulation as if one could keep the other person confused and out of balance, so to speak, they are unable to protect themselves from confusion tactics.

Interruptions

You can interrupt and redirect behaviors - the surprise that is likely to happen when you suddenly interrupt someone is usually enough opening to suggest you do something else, which it likely will.

Scarcity and regret

One of the easiest ways to create something more valuable is to limit it - once it's no longer unlimited, everyone wants it and everyone will fight for a piece of it. This means that you can get people to want something or do something just by limiting their choices. You can tell someone not to do something, which makes them more likely to do it out of spite, or you can limit their choices, making them feel like they should act or regret not doing it in the first place.

Advanced Behavioral Anchoring

This refers to the idea that you can create biases that affect a person about how they behave through an anchor. For example, when making decisions, you typically rely on an anchor of information. This anchor is used as your prejudice for whatever you decide. For example, if you need to decide what types of crops your farm will grow, you would anchor yourself to specific information about what grows well in your area. This can then be hijacked, however, if someone instills a fake anchor. If someone convinces you that bananas grow well in your climate rather than the usual cotton you grow, you may be making decisions based on that imperfect anchor that told you to grow bananas. This means that if you can instill false anchors in someone else, you can make sure they behave in ways that are relevant to you and benefit you. Using the voice

Your voice is perhaps the most influential and convincing tool of all - your tone can get people to do a wide variety of things. Think about it this way: you're much more likely to accept something if someone asks politely than if they yelled at you or sang it to you. For example, if you're trying to get someone else's attention, you can lower your voice to a whisper to get their attention. Suddenly they will have to listen carefully and focus on you and what you are saying to hear you, and they will. You can lead people based on your tone and how strong or soft, energetic or gentle you do.

Chapter 2: Observing Human Behavior

Observation is a process of observing, or studying, something to gain insights or information about it. The quickest and most effective way to get to know something or someone is to observe them with an objective mind. While this may seem easy, to truly observe someone and learn, you need to be completely objective and put aside any prejudices or prejudices you may already have. The good news is that perception can be improved with repetition, dedication, and rapid, replicable learning. In this chapter we will cover the basics.

Improving your observation skills can help you improve communication and can also tell you about events, people and the world around you. Learning and applying observation skills can make us adapt faster and can also make us emotionally connect with others, contributing to a mutually beneficial outcome. You can use your observation skills to not only study people, but also to help make life decisions. Below we will cover a range of observation and related skills to assist you with the rest of the content in this book.

Basic Observation Skills:

An easy way to practice your observation skills is to do something that you find important or interesting. Pick one thing to focus on and ignore what is not directly related to that object. Challenge yourself to focus on something new every day. It could be something you find fascinating or just a random item you choose to look for. You could spend the whole day looking for stained glass windows in buildings as you walk down the street. You may be looking for a certain make or model of a car when sitting in traffic on your way to work. When you see an improvement in your abilities, select a smaller object or item that may be more difficult and see what you can discern from it.

When you observe human behavior, observe how people speak, what mannerisms they use and how they communicate with others. Next time you take a lunch break, take some time to observe your colleagues or the people around you, spending a good 10 to 30 minutes each day if possible. The more you practice, the faster you will learn. As your skills increase, your challenges should also increase. Set specific challenges and goals for yourself, such as memorizing specific details, observing multiple things at once, and comparing the daily behaviors of the people around you.

Memorization skills:

Although modern technology makes it easy for you to take notes, you will find it difficult to use it to help you when you are in intense social situations. Expanding and improving your short-term memory will help you use all the information you have gathered. We will describe a couple of techniques to improve it.

Take a picture. This photo can be an image of your set or a commercial. Spend a few moments analyzing this image and taking everything you can remember from the photo. Flip the image over, then try to remember every detail you might have. Write down or mention the elements that are in the context of the photo, the clothes people are wearing, the weather, and similar information. Make it a regular part of your schedule, take the time to improve your skills and move on to more complex imagery once you've mastered the basics.

You may have played a kid's game where you had cards with an animal image on one side and a blank face on the other. The game was played by placing the cards face down, then turning two cards over to try to find the matching pair of animals. The aim of the game was to match each mother animal with the cub. Players had to remember where the cards were so that they could match as many pairs as possible during their turn. While this game may seem childish today, it is a great test of memory and observation. There are several apps, of different quality, that can be found for mobile devices similar to this one and can help you if you are short on time or physical materials.

Similar to the animal game, there is another similar game called "spot the difference". The aim of this game is as follows: you are presented with two images of a very similar nature and you need to determine what small differences exist between the two images. Some of the differences may be obvious, and some of the differences require some acute observation skills to be detected. Spot the Difference games are also known as children's games and can be found in many children's magazines and books. However, the game is also a favorite among adults. The books that include this game are still published today, and there are also phone apps you can download that include some challenging photos that require focus and concentration.

Logical and analytical skills:

Equally important and complementary to your observation skills should be your logical and analytical skills.

Logical thinking is one of the most important skills you can learn, from analyzing human behavior to planning what to do with your time, to considering your views on different topics. The fictional detective, Sherlock Holmes, used observations to make logical inferences and deductions and relied heavily on the Scottish medical school teacher and Queen Victoria's personal surgeon, Joseph Bell. Like Bell and his counterpart Holmes, you can be a master of everything you observe. You can start making logical statements based on what you have observed, which you can test. Keep a written record when you practice the observation skills written above and take a look at them. Try to link them together.

For example, suppose you observe the following:

1. A colleague sometimes fidgets with his hands
2. They change the subject when they discuss a certain person
3. They shake their hands when they talk about a certain person You can infer the following:

    I. According to statement 2, the colleague does not want to waste time talking about this person

    II. Based on statements 3 and I, coworker shakes hands when talking about someone they don't want to waste time talking about

    III. Based on statements 1 and II, the colleague may be waving their hands when talking about something, or someone they don't want to waste time thinking about

Using your observations you can determine the body language cues on your co-worker and use them to take a course of action. In this case perhaps; avoid talking about this specific person if you want to avoid confrontation; further discuss the person to understand why the colleague is behaving this way; looking for more things the colleague will change the subject about and seeing if they too are agitated to confirm what you saw and to learn more about them.

While not necessarily that fun, math problems require a lot of attention, concentration, and logical thinking. Practicing math skills allows you to focus and can be monumental in helping you improve your analytical skills as math requires solid logical deduction skills. You need to pay attention to every step of the process - missing a logical step results in incorrect answers. Reading math books, like Euclid's Elements, can be time-consuming, but it's an incredibly useful way to test your analytical skills while giving you the basics of logical thinking.

Additional skills:

In addition to all these methods to improve your observation skills, you can help your observation skills by taking care of your mind and body. These additional aids can be farmed and used to cultivate your skills, and even in a short time, you can see improvements.

Avoiding distractions:

You can't properly focus on what's going on around you if you're on your phone, checking Facebook or Instagram every few minutes, or texting your friends every other minute. Not only do you waste your time on your phone as you slowly walk around the store, others are forced to turn around you - rude behavior. The result is that you are unable to focus on what is happening around you or give yourself the opportunity to observe people and situations. To take advantage of what you have learned, minimize distractions when in public places and stay away from the phone. You will be amazed at how much more you realize when you can devote your full attention to what surrounds you.

Short breaks:

Taking a short break, to refocus or just to get up and walk around for a couple of minutes, can be monumental for keeping your mind sharp. Taking a ten minute break gives your brain a chance to adapt and focus on something else so that when you get back to work with a fresh frame of mind.

Verbal observations:

Time to look for a practical way to apply your knowledge. "Sticks and stones can break my bones, but words will never hurt me." A common phrase in a schoolyard that many grew up listening to. Ultimately it is the basis of how words can only influence us if we choose to leave them. In fact, a person's words often reveal a lot about their personality and character. To provide observation examples we will list some words and show examples of how words can be interpreted.

"Another":

Let's say you've just met someone and one of the first things you hear is "someone else". It could be used in many different sentences. For example, "I got another job offer" or "I just got another call". Using this word, you can infer that this person is used to receiving job offers, meaning, is or appears to be a highly sought after person. Also, by using this specific word, the person subconsciously expresses that they want you to know how important, popular or desired they are. Using other observations on this person you could deduce a couple of scenarios.

Primarily, this could be used to improve their self-esteem, and as with most people using this term, they feel the need for others to know, so that they can have a better sense of self-worth. Try to remember if they are easily embarrassed or if they have difficulty presenting their ideas in large groups.

Second, they might use it as a way to get your attention, a way to get noticed and get your respect and admiration. Try to remember if they have recently sought more attention, especially around you or a certain group of people. This will confirm what you have learned.

"Hard":

This person could use this word in several ways. For example, they might say things like "I worked hard to get to where I am today" or "I worked very hard to get what I have". This gives you an immediate indication that this person, despite how little you know about them, appreciates goals that require a hard work ethic. We can also infer that this person appreciates the things that can be achieved through hard work and dedication. Moreover, based on their use of this word, it can also be understood that this person believes that dedication and perseverance in hard work leads to positive results.

Alternatively, this could be used in the opposite context, such as "This job is really hard" or, "Why is it so hard to make friends?". Pay attention to the context and other details. Aren't they working hard? This clearly shows someone who is lazy or, at least, doesn't seem to want to make any effort. Are they determined but they can't seem to get it to work? They are likely frustrated by their lack of understanding despite their best efforts.

"Patiently":

First, the person you are communicating with and trying to analyze might say something like, "I patiently took the test" or "I have been patiently sitting in a traffic jam, waiting my turn." In fact, they were involved in what was going on, which is why they were "patiently" waiting for whatever happened at that moment. In reality it is exactly the opposite! The term is seen as more sarcasm or impatience in how, during the incident, they were really focusing or wanted to be in a completely different place. Pointing out that they waited passively indicates that this incident (or whatever happened) was terrible because the whole time they were worried about where they wanted to go or what else they had to do.

On the other hand, this type of phrase also tells you that whoever you speak feels strongly obeying social norms and being polite. Although they found the task or event time-consuming, boring, or unworthy of their time, especially since they had to be somewhere else or some other commitment to strive for, they still waited for the event to end. See if you can remember if this person reacts similarly during other social situations.

"Decided":

If a person often makes announcements like "I decided to buy the blue one instead of the green one", you can infer that he is the type of person who takes into account various forms of choice and looks at all the pros and cons of a situation before taking. a decision.

You can determine that this is the type of person who takes things seriously, even minor decisions, by reflecting and weighing all their options. Think about the other choices they have made and the time it takes them to make them.

You can also conclude the opposite by using this term. In other words, this person is not the type to make reckless and impulsive decisions. It is very common for introverted people to have thought processes where they are very careful about reflecting on things, weigh all options and are very careful in their decision making, so if you notice that this person is more reserved in social situations, this can be the case.

"Right":

With this word, you can easily begin to identify a person's opinions (and how it affects their personality) about personal, moral or ethical dilemmas and even what they do when it comes to these situations.

If a person tells you, "I chose the right one" or "it was the right thing to do", you can easily determine that this person takes into account the legal, moral, ethical and personal values they hold before making a choice or decision.

This should show you that this person has strong personality traits and that they actively choose to make choices based on these priorities. In general, if a person uses this term in multiple sentences in your conversations, you can tell that they have a strong moral compass.

As you can see above, words have power, especially in the hands of a good listener. As always, context is key when interpreting other people's words, so always make sure to use as many methods as possible before coming to a firm conclusion. The more data you have, the better the judgment you can make.

Body and behavioral observation:

Now that we've explored the basics of verbal observation, it's time to look at some basic body language examples. To recap, when a person acts it is a reflection of how he was raised, his social influences combined with how this manifests itself through universal human expressions. Most of the time they respond unconsciously, without realizing it. You can begin to determine how your peers' actions reveal information about their family and home life.

Humans engage in biologically, socially and intellectually influenced behaviors. These behaviors are encouraged and influenced by many external sources, such as culture, age groups, peers, religious beliefs, ethnicity and emotions. Some behaviors help us live and evolve, while others are harmful.

Aggressive behavior can, unfortunately, be a common occurrence for many people in their life. Historically, the justifications for the attack have been varied. 17th-century philosopher Thomas Hobbes believed that violent behavior occurs for three reasons: competition, mistrust, or glory. In the justification of self-preservation, violence could be used to subjugate others, face threats or assert social domination. In contrast, the philosopher Rousseau believed that humans were naturally kind and compassionate animals and that temperament and hatred were learned behaviors. In the 20th century, various psychological and genetic experiments determined the physiological and genetic components of aggression. Soviet geneticist Dmitry K. Belyaev conducted several genetic experiments on non-domesticated foxes in the 1950's in an attempt to study the effects of selective breeding on friendliness in a species and whether this could explain the domestication of canine species. Barring the violent and aggressive foxes, he found that later generations exhibited more social behavior and even began to exhibit physical characteristics similar to domestic dogs, such as floppy ears, curled tails, star-shaped fur patterns on the head, and features more feminine.

Crucially, the fox researchers also found that more sociable animals had higher base levels of serotonin than their more aggressive counterparts. Current research from leading universities has found that serotonin mediates interactions between the prefrontal cortex (involved in higher decision making) and the amygdala (involved in basic brain function and emotions) and, although it is a subject of debate, it is thought that it is easier to regulate the emotional response such as aggression. What this research tells us is that aggression is partly determined by genetics, but also that aggressive behavior can manifest itself in physical traits and behaviors.

Aggressive behavior is seen at a time when people feel cornered or threatened. It could be a response to fear or a reaction to perceived injustice. When the body experiences emotions of fear or anger, there are certain physiological changes that you can observe when a person enters the commonly known "fight or flight" response.

Rapid breathing:
Feeling that quick action may need to be taken, the body increases the respiratory rate to increase the amount of oxygen available to the body. Lung capacity has also been found to increase in these situations.

Eye dilation:

The body responds in the fight or flight state to increase the dilation of the pupils in your eyes by releasing the aforementioned stress hormones. Keep in mind that while this is a symptom of aggressive intent, it can also be observed when someone is attracted to you.

Trembling:

As the body prepares, it will divert resources to the muscles in anticipation of further action. This causes tremors, as the muscles experience low-level contractions due to increased blood flow and nerve response.

Pale skin:

As the body prepares for battle or retreat, it scales the delivery of important resources from the extremities to the muscles to prepare them. Lack of blood in the skin will give this individual a pale appearance.

Be very aware that while the above are physical signs of aggression, the "fight or flight" response is also used when a person is anxious or scared. The "flight" is there for a reason. Be sure to put their actions in context when making a judgment about their temperament. Someone who shivers, blushes, and breathes rapidly may simply be anxious about their situation and may not be physically invasive of your space or use aggressive language.

This is where the behavior comes into focus. After looking at physiological behaviors, you can take a look at some common aggressive behaviors.

Invasion of personal space:

A clear sign of domination, or aggression, is moving into someone's space. What is the space that differs from person to person, but close contact and rapid physical movement and touch indicate that a person does not take this into account.

Speech aloud:

Shouting is a classic aggressive behavior. It allows a person to assert dominance and anger without having to resort to physical means and clearly announces displeasure.

Depending on the person, this can be more subtle than just bellowing across the room. A more passive aggressive person may raise their voice noticeably but not scream or, in fact, become so quiet to silence in situations where their feedback is crucial.

Standing proud:

An outwardly aggressive person is much more likely to stand up and expose their chest. Looking bigger than their attacker and asserting physical strength are the main goals, similar to fighting wolves in the wild. The classic signs are to have the shoulders pushed back, to stand straight, to pose with the legs apart and to keep the head up.

Emotional observation:

When deciphering someone's emotions, first remember what their foundation is. Does this person usually behave this way or act out of the ordinary? Is their emotional state positive or negative? Consider false positives, such as when someone just got promoted or if a close relative has just died. So admit they may feel hurt or lonely when this action is negative.

Happiness:

Seeing someone feel joy, especially when they are a child, brings joy. Happiness is considered a contagious emotion and is the most sought after. Here are some very interesting human behaviors to think about. Why do humans kiss? Well, clearly, because it feels good, but is it a learned or instinctive behavior? Some anthropologists suggest that kisses could be traced back to our ancient ancestors, who passed chewed food to their babies by the lips, and that the feeling of kissing is comforting. Others who claim this action is learned point out that remote tribes also engage in the behavior.

Dancing:

Why do people dance? Dancing and vaulting have been around since the dawn of time and can be found anywhere in the world. Some animals have also been observed dancing. Research published in the Public Library of Science's Journal of Genetics in 2006 reported that dance may have been linked to survival long ago. It was a means of communicating and connecting with others. Dancing may also have been used to attract a mate, for example the way people are attracted to dancing nowadays, such as at parties.

Cry:

Have you ever wondered why negative emotions lead to crying? Why do people cry? Crying is a very beautiful part of being human and it is a very unique behavior. Seeing someone cry can make us cry too, and humans naturally feel pain for others. Crying is triggered by our body's "fight or flight" systems. The limbic system of the human brain, consisting of the amygdala, hippocampus, and hypothalamus, regulates daily human behaviors and emotions. This system is connected by nerves to the tear ducts (or tear glands) in the eye and, when you are distressed or experiencing negative emotions, it causes you to start crying.

When we cry, non-verbally communicate to anyone who sees that you are emotionally hurt. Imagine the last big disappointment in your life and how you felt in that moment. Your pulse is likely racing, you may be sweating, have a lump in your throat, or are feeling low on energy. All of these things are affected by the buildup of cortisol, the stress hormone, in your body. Crying can help reduce cortisol levels in the body by releasing adrenocorticotropic hormone, a chemical element of cortisol, the stress hormone, into the tears that flow down the face. After crying, you will usually feel less stressed or slightly drained.

When you analyze your supervisor, colleague or colleague to try to understand others, you will need to let go of your stereotypes. As far as the mind can judge, you must be able to let go of rigid and fixed ideas. People who read others well are certainly qualified to interpret the invisible, invisible social connections that guide our daily life.

Now that we have covered observation techniques, we will spend the next three chapters covering the three main techniques we will use to analyze human behavior: body language, intuition, and emotional intelligence.

Chapter 3 Body Language Basic

Body language refers to non-verbal communication that can be inferred from a person's behavior or conduct. Body language, therefore, negates the element of oral communication whereby a person does not have to say what they have in mind. However, the same can be inferred from their observable conduct. One of the reasons why understanding body language is so essential is the fact that people rarely say what they have in mind during normal conversation, and as such, understanding body language will allow you to know exactly how it feels. another person on a problem. Sometimes, you may find yourself faced with a situation where you need to formulate an appropriate response to a problem that is affecting someone else. However, you cannot respond appropriately if you are unable to accurately understand their point of view. Understanding body language allows you to find an adequate response to various situations that interest our friends and colleagues. Therefore, you will end up forming good relationships with the people around you, as they will feel that you understand their situation.

One of the most important things you should remember when it comes to body language and communication in general is that non-verbal communication makes up more than 60 percent of all communication. This implies that if you are able to understand body language, you will be able to access more information about other people, their concerns, fears and motivations. This makes you a better communicator, as well as improving your overall leadership skills.

How to read body language

Knowing how to read other people and respond to them is the ultimate skill when it comes to understanding body language. There are many ways people communicate and that may not necessarily involve teaching using words. This, therefore, implies that other parts of the body, such as the eyes, arms, feet and facial expression, also play a key role when it comes to body language in general.

Focus on the eyes

Focusing on the eyes can be very helpful when it comes to your ability to understand body language. The behavior of another person with respect to the position of the feet, the nature of the handshake, the position of the hands and arms, and the movements of the eyes, including the size of the pupil, can tell you exactly how they feel about the problem in question. .

Visual contact

Direct eye contact is an indicator that the person you are communicating with is interested in whatever you want to say. On the other hand, the inability to make direct eye contact means that the person is likely not interested in the topic of the conversation. Additionally, the lack of direct eye contact can also imply that the person is dishonest or uncomfortable with the conversation you are having with them. For example, they may view the topic of conversation as a taboo and an issue they may not be willing to discuss openly.

Flashing frequency

When it comes to the eyes, another key aspect of body language is the blinking of the eye. The blink rate that stays within the normal range is a likely indicator that someone is relaxed and has nothing to hide. However, a higher than normal blink rate reveals that the person you are communicating with may be extremely stressed and uncomfortable with the situation. You should always make sure that you are able to focus on the blink rate so that you know exactly the position, worries or fears the other person might be feeling.

Dilation of pupils

Pupil dilation is also something that can let you know if the other person is genuinely interested in you or not. Pupil dilation is an indicator that the person is taking an interest in what you are saying. If the person is not interested in the topic of the conversation, the learner size is likely to remain the same.

Ultimately, the eyes play a crucial role when it comes to body language and non-verbal communication. Sometimes, someone might tell you something, but their eyes seem to be saying something completely different. By focusing on eye behavior, including dilation of the pupils, the blink rate between things will allow you to get a more accurate picture of the true position that is held by the person you are communicating with.

Head movement and body language

Head movement is also another element of body language that can offer highly reliable information regarding the exact position and feeling the other person has towards you or the topic under discussion. The speed at which a person nods during a conversation can let you know whether or not the person is interested in the conversation or disinterested in it. Nodding

Quickly nodding during a conversation is a likely indicator that the person you're communicating with isn't really interested in the conversation. A quick nod is very often a sign of impatience on the part of the other person, so they would prefer you to speed up the conversation and get to the end of the main point. On the other hand, a slow nod of the head is a sign of genuine interest. Slowly nodding could indicate that the person has taken a deep interest in what you are saying and wants to know more.

Head tilt

During a conversation, you may notice that the person you are communicating with is tilting their head towards you or away from you. Tilting your head towards you is an indicator that the other person trusts you and believes what you are saying. However, if they tend to tilt their heads away from you then this is an indicator that the person you are communicating with does not trust what you are saying as they may have doubts about it.

Also, you can always tell another person's perception of you by simply focusing on their body language and, in particular, their head. This is particularly applicable during a group conversation. If someone seems to be leaning towards you or looking in your direction during a group conversation, then that's a sign that they seem to be taking you seriously in terms of what you are saying. Alternatively, if they don't look in your direction or appear to be doing so for an extremely short period of time, then this is an indicator that they probably aren't taking you seriously.

Focus on the movement of the hand and arm

Concealment of hands and use of gestures

Hand and arm behavior are key components of body language during normal conversation. Starting with the hands, hiding your hands by putting them in your pocket is a sign that the other person is dishonest or that they are nervous. A normal conversation should, therefore, involve exposing the hands as this is an indicator that someone actually has nothing to hide. For example, if you happen to have a conversation with another person and they put both hands on the table during the conversation, then this is an indicator that they have nothing to hide. The use of hand gestures is also something you should pay attention to when it comes to body language communication. For example, pointing hands at a specific individual during a group conversation is a likely indicator that the speaker has a high affinity for the individual in question.

Hands over your mouth

Sometimes you may notice someone trying to cover their mouth during a conversation. This form of body language is mainly used when someone tries to be discreet about something. However, covering your mouth during a conversation can also indicate that the person may not necessarily be telling the truth.

Crossing the arms

In addition to the hands, the arms also play a key role in body language and non-verbal communication. Crossing the arms is considered to be one of the most notable aspects of body language. When someone crosses their arms across their chest, they are more likely to be defensive and less likely to tolerate the idea of opening up about their personal life. Crossed arms, therefore, are considered to be some sort of black road that the other person is subtly letting you know that they are unwilling to let you in. However, in certain situations, crossed arms can be a sign of self-confidence on the other person's side. This is especially true if the person crosses their arms over their chest, but at the same time she is apparently overly relaxed and willing to share as much information with you as possible. You should, therefore,

Arms on hips

When it comes to the arms, positioning the arms on the hip area is a vital aspect of body language. Most of the time, placing the arms in the hip area is considered an attempt to establish dominance of the other person. This behavior is mostly observed by people with authority in both the social and professional spheres.

Body proximity

You can tell a lot about how another person feels about you or the topic you are discussing based on how close they are to you during your interaction. Closeness to the body refers to the physical closeness a person is willing to have with you during a conversation. Proximity can relate to both the sitting and standing positions of the other person in the course of your interaction with them.

In general, when someone is willing to stand or sit next to you while you interact with them, they likely see you as someone they can establish a substantial relationship with. It can be a business relationship, a cordial friendship, or even a romantic relationship. On the other hand, if the person prefers to keep their distance while interacting with you, this can be an indicator that they are not really into you. However, it's important to point out that proximity to the body is something that may differ from one culture to another. For example, in some cultures, men are not allowed to stand or sit next to women in public, even if they are husband and wife. In such societies, proximity may not offer the most accurate interpretation of body language.

Facial expression

The facial expression someone has while interacting with them can let you know if they like you or not. A smile is perhaps the best indicator when it comes to facial expression and its general implication as body language. When he smiles at you during a conversation, he is most likely telling you that he is having a good time and looks like he is enjoying your company. However, if someone insists on keeping a serious look during a conversation, they are probably not enjoying your company and may prefer to be left alone.

When it comes to facial expression, and especially smiling, it's important to know how to distinguish between a genuine smile and a fake smile. A genuine smile is usually a form of dilation of the eyes and also of the entire face. On the other hand, a fake smile may not be visible in the eyes as it is centered only in the mouth area. This, therefore, implies that it is very difficult for someone to hide their true feelings with a smile if they know exactly what to look for.

The positioning of the feet

Most of the time, people focus on controlling their facial expressions but forget about the feet. For this reason, focusing on foot movement could be very reliable if you're trying to study the body language of the person next to you. The movement of the feet can have various interpretations depending on the exact situation in which you are engaged. In a one-on-one conversation, footwork can let you know if a person is looking favorably on you or not. If the person seems to be pointing their feet at you, then this is an indicator that you probably like them and they will likely pay more attention to what you have to say.

In the case of a group conversation, focusing on other people's feet could offer insightful information about where their loyalty or true feelings really lie. For example, someone might watch you interact with you in a group chat. However, you do realize that while they are talking to you, their legs seem to be pointing towards someone else. As much as they seem to be focusing on you, their real target is the person that their feet are facing this likely indicator. A good example would be in an office where one of the junior employees is talking to a senior employee with his or her feet pointing in the direction of another senior employee. The general implication is that, ultimately, their loyalty rests with the senior employee towards whom they have placed their feet.

Nature of the handshake

Handshakes are considered the most common way to greet and recognize other people. However, handshakes are also important when it comes to body language. A firm handshake usually means that you are interacting with someone who has high self-esteem and who is likely to be a reliable ally. On the other hand, a weak handshake could indicate that the person has low self-esteem and may be unreliable.

When it comes to the handshake, some people usually insist on tilting the other person's hand so that their hand ends up on top. These people are likely to be control freaks who would insist on doing what they want during a negotiation.

Importance of body language

Very few people have embraced the habit of saying exactly what they have in mind. Some people actually say one thing while, in essence, they mean the exact opposite. A better understanding of body language is very important in letting you know exactly what another person thinks about you or the topic under discussion. When you fully understand body language, you can find an appropriate answer. Many times, cases of miscommunication usually occur when people cannot read and respond to body language. For example, you could present a business idea to a potential client and they tell you they like the idea. However, you realize later that they are unwilling or hesitant to assist you. In such a scenario,

In the above scenario, if you happen to have a good grasp of the concept of body language, you may have noticed elements of non-verbal conversation that would have indicated how they truly felt about your proposal. For example, they may have indicated that they like the proposal, but during the conversation you notice that they are moving away from you. Similarly, the customer or potential business partner may have acted surprised and even smiled at the idea, but it is noted that the pupil dilation is zero.

Having an understanding of body language can also help you avoid embarrassing situations. For example, you might meet someone for the first time and they smile at you as they favor you. You decide to go ahead and ask them on a date only to realize they aren't interested in you. A good understanding of body language would have allowed you to notice subtle signs such as their tendency to keep some distance from you during conversations. With this knowledge, you can avoid embarrassing situations that could arise due to misinterpretation of body language.

A good understanding of body language can also help you avoid inadvertently sending the wrong message to someone. This is particularly the case when you interact with someone from a different socio-cultural background. You may be from a society where physical closeness, especially between members of the opposite sex, is not encouraged. However, you meet someone you like and insist on keeping a considerable distance from them as you interact. The other person is likely to misinterpret your body language and conclude that you don't like it when, in fact, you do.

Chapter 4 How to find out if you are manipulated

Have you ever felt a sudden lack of confidence in yourself or, worse, this curious and distressing feeling of not knowing how to communicate? Have you ever been deafened by doubts about your abilities or qualities? Have you ever been inhabited by that feeling of inferiority that paralyzes you, makes your blood run cold and prevents you from reacting normally? If you have ever experienced this type of situation, it is because you have been the victim of type III manipulation and placed in the line of sight of a manipulator. Recall that the second type of manipulator is a selfish or self-centered person who thinks only of his interests, without worrying about the consequences. But the type III manipulator, also called manipulator, has a very different characteristic intention. Its only goal is to destroy. Everything he undertakes is aimed at killing you, ruining what you do or destroying an aspect of your personality that does not suit him. The manipulator is characterized both by his willingness to harm and by a formidable capacity for concealment. This is why many people don't trust him or take him for another.

The manipulator shows no distinctive signs and his perversity is not necessarily read on his face. It is a true chameleon who hides behind deceptive appearances to destroy better. It can take the form of an "overprotective" parent who, out of selfishness, prevents the child from becoming independent. The manipulator could be a nice grandmother who secretly gives money to her little girl who is in rehab to, presumably, "help her hold on." It can also be a mistress, lover, boss, neighbor, teacher, or longtime friend. In the welcoming atmosphere of the offices, he is the co-worker willing to do anything to take your place or that colleague who tries to devalue you because your competence is shady. He plans to destroy. Sometimes it can bring him something,

1. Manipulators play on fear.

Most manipulators will emphasize specific points and exaggerate the facts to scare you and make you act the way they want. The way to identify this game is to look for statements that imply that you are not strong or brave enough or that if you miss out on one thing in particular, you are a loser.

2. Manipulators deceive

Everyone values honesty and transparency, so they will avoid deceivers. Manipulators understand this concept and are very cunning when they lie. They twist the facts or try to show you only the side of the story that benefits them. For example, a co-worker may spread some unconfirmed rumors to take over. To avoid being deceived, don't believe everything you hear. Instead, base your choices on credible sources and ask questions if the details aren't clear.

3. Manipulators take advantage of your happiness

Have you noticed that you are more likely to say yes to anything when you are happy or in a good mood? When we are happy, we tend to take opportunities that look good even before we think about things. Master manipulators have this knowledge so they will take advantage of the moods. To manage this emotional opportunity and avoid manipulation, work on improving awareness of your emotions, both positive and negative. strive to find a balance between logic and emotions when making decisions.

4. Manipulators benefit from reciprocity.

Do you know that feeling you get when you owe someone a favor, especially if they've helped you at some point? That feeling of debt makes you vulnerable. It's hard to say no to a manipulator if you owe him something. Most manipulators will try to butter and flatter you with small favors, so ask for a big one in return. While giving brings more joy than receiving, knowing your limitations is more important. Don't be afraid to say no when you have to, even if you owe someone a favor.

5. Manipulators push for an advantage on the field at home

It is very easy to convince a person when you are in a familiar place. As such, a manipulator will push you to meet in a familiar place while you are not. Ownership gives power and comfort, so a place like home or office will provide the manipulator with some authority. You will need to make meeting requests in a neutral place where familiarity and ownership are diluted to disarm the manipulator.

6. The manipulator will ask many questions.

Of course it's easy to talk about yourself. Master manipulators know this; so they take advantage of it to ask some in-depth questions. Their schedules are hidden, but basically they try to uncover your weaknesses or other information they may hold against you. Of course, it would be unfair of you to assume that everyone has the wrong motives because there are some people who genuinely try to get to know you better. However, it's okay to question people, especially those who don't reveal anything about themselves.

7. The manipulator will speak quickly

To manipulate you through your emotions, the manipulator will speak quickly and sometimes use special jargon and vocabulary. This will give them an advantage because you won't have enough time to think. To counteract this form of manipulation, don't be afraid to ask for some time to process what the person said. Also, try to ask the person to repeat any unclear statements. To gain some control over a conversation, repeat the other person's affirmations in your own words and let them sink in.

8. The display of negative emotions

Some manipulators will use tones of voice to control your emotions. The tone and body language most commonly used by manipulators are negative. For example, basketball coaches (they use manipulation for positive purposes) are masters at raising their voices and using strong body language to manipulate players' emotions. To avoid such manipulation, you should practice pausing. It's about taking a break from the conversation or situation and having some time to think before reacting. You can step away for a few minutes to control your emotions.

9.   Manipulators limit your time to act

Every manipulator wants to win. They can do this by making sure you don't have enough time to think. For example, a person could force you to make a serious decision in an unreasonably limited amount of time. He / she will try to guide your thoughts to their advantage. You won't have enough time to weigh the consequences. To avoid a situation where you give up without thinking about it, don't be in a hurry to submit. Make sure the question is reasonable. Take a break, ask for some time, and if the person doesn't allow you to think, walk away. You will be happier looking for everything you need elsewhere.

10. The treatment of silence.

According to Preston Ni, a manipulator will assume power in a relationship by making you wait. For example, when a person deliberately does not respond to your reasonable messages, calls, emails or other questions, they make you wait and, at the same time, place uncertainty and doubt in your mind. Some manipulators use silence as a lever. To avoid being a victim of manipulation through the silent treatment, give people deadlines and don't allow them to intimidate you. For example, after trying to communicate to a reasonable extent, let the mother go and let the other person approach.

Manipulators will work to raise their emotional awareness to gain the upper hand over others. A large number of people are learning how to be emotionally intelligent. You too should try to hone your emotional intelligence levels for your protection.

Personality types are described as psychological classifications given to individuals with specific behavioral patterns and tendencies. Companies and organizations have begun to incorporate personality tests to designate individuals to specific functions or job roles within the organization based on their test results.

The Myers-Briggs Personality Type Indicator is one of the most commonly used tests to understand what everyone's personality is.

According to the Myers-Briggs indicator, there are 16 different personality types. The very fact that there are 16 types in the Myers-Briggs indicator shows how complex people are and how their emotions and behaviors are all different to varying degrees. To analyze body language and learn to recognize the warning signs of lies and deceptions through non-verbal communication, there are four main personality categories you need to focus on:

Peaceful personalities - They are patient, diplomatic, easy-going and prefer to avoid confrontations with people. This group prefers to have order and peace and thrive better in this type of environment. They are known to be very simple people and are quite emotionally stable. They bring balance to companies that are fast and have the strengths to build a work team. Due to their nature, it is generally easier to spot the telltale signs of a lie when it happens, as peaceful personalities are often uncomfortable with being deceptive. They encourage respect, value and harmony between people in the workplace.

Playful Personalities: These individuals are fairly easy to recognize. They are fun, energetic, enthusiastic, loud and are generally considered to be outgoing and love to socialize with people. They have a lot of ideas, are innovative, creative and work fast, but the downside is that sometimes these types of creatives tend to be disorganized. Not all playful personalities will be your friends, though, and if someone is too friendly in certain situations like work (especially if you've just met them), be on the lookout, they may not be trustworthy. Playful personalities prefer affection, approval, and attention.

Influential Personalities - These confident and in control individuals are generally both authoritative and productive. It is known that most of the people classified under this personality do not give up easily. They like to take control and face every situation head on. They have high inner strength and usually stop at nothing until their goals have been achieved. This competitive streak, however, tends to bring out some less than pleasant qualities, depending on the individual in question. Some may have no qualms about having to resort to lies and deceit if it means they can move on. These personality types are attracted to credit, loyalty, and appreciation.

Precise personalities - Precise personalities are perfectionists. They value order, as well as structure and compliance. They are organized, they put their work before play or social life and stop working only until they have finished their tasks. Typically, these personality types prefer space to work alone, choosing calm and sensitivity over chaos and disorganization. Before you can start analyzing someone else's personality type based on their body language, you first need to understand your personality. From the friends you choose to the job you do, the passions you have, and even the candidates you vote for, it all comes down to your personality. Your personality influences almost every major area of your life and the decisions you make. By understanding your personality, you get a better insight into what your strengths and weaknesses are. It helps you develop an understanding of how the people around you perceive you. How you interact with others will inevitably affect their body language to some extent as well. Psychologists have classified personality types into five main categories, known as The Five-Factor Model. They believe that each of us has some degree of these characteristics within our personality.

Openness - Having a wide range of interests and a vivid imagination could mean that you have high levels of openness in your personality. People with this personality trait are creative and curious, preferring variety to stiffness. Open individuals pursue self-realization through euphoric and intense experiences, such as living abroad, for example, or going on self-discovery missions. Sometimes, they can be seen as unpredictable and blurry.

Conscientiousness: Generally known to be reliable, efficient, well-organized, and self-reliant, these personality types prefer to plan their day and tasks and always aim for better results. That is, if you have a high level of conscientiousness in your personality. At the other end of the spectrum, those with low levels of conscientiousness are usually seen as obsessive and stubborn.

Extroversion - Those with high levels of extroversion in their personality thrive in social activity. You could also say they are social butterflies. They are outgoing, talkative and have no problem being in the spotlight. At times, this can be seen as attention seeking and overbearing. Pleasantness - Being pleasant makes you kind, trustworthy and affectionate towards people. Those with sympathetic personalities are known for their prosocial behavior and are engaged in altruistic activities and volunteer work. Some people may perceive this personality trait as naive and overly passive.

Neuroticism: High levels of neuroticism in your personality could mean that you are considered "emotionally unstable". Tendencies in this personality trait include being reactive and excitable, but that also means they have a greater ability to experience unpleasant emotions such as irritability, insecurity, and anxiety.

We pay too much attention to the words we hear and not enough attention to what we should observe. While we can't deny that verbal communication is an important skill set to have, becoming a truly effective communicator means you need to take your skills one step further by learning to understand unspoken language. Your main goal in learning to read body language is to determine how honest and genuine people are with you. It's the only way to decipher someone's innermost thoughts and get to the truth.

There are several contexts in which being able to analyze body language will prove to be a useful skill. Job interviews, conflict resolution, maybe even when you have to solve a crime. People can lie and they can do it right. They can tell you anything you want to hear. But even though we may have been able to trick our mind into saying words we don't mean, we still can't fool our body into running the perfect lie, and this is your window of opportunity to seek the truth by looking below, the surface to see the truth.

Body language is communication in its most honest and genuine form. Research conducted in this area reveals that the things we feel tend to manifest first in the body and only seconds later in the conscious mind. This means that when these thoughts have reached your mind, it is often too late as your body may have already betrayed you. An effective body language analysis must consider all factors present, including the context in which the interaction occurs.

Common signs of body language

As we get older, we (unfortunately) become more adept at lying and masking our true emotions or intentions. Only verbally, though, because our bodies aren't on board yet. The brain is programmed to want to read the emotions of others. This is one of the reasons empathy is considered an emotional intelligence skill because we inherently want to empathize and share what we think someone else might be going through. This is part of our evolution and we have developed this need out of necessity for our survival. When we see someone showing fear, we know instinctively and immediately how to react. We know what actions need to be taken and this approach can also be applied to other aspects of body language analysis.

There are several categories of body language signals that we can learn to analyze:

Aggression: Dazzling, frowning anger visible on the face, threatening approach, clenched fists, clenched jaw, and attempting to tower over you are signs that someone is exhibiting aggressive body language tendencies. Dominance - When an individual wants to be in charge or in control of the situation, they will demonstrate dominant body language cues to signal this inner desire. An example of what dominant body language looks like can be found in confident individuals who often stand with their swollen chest outward as a way to express this dominance.

Bored - These indicators are easy enough to spot, but again, the context in which it is occurring needs to be kept in mind. Poor eye contact and repetitive yawning are indicators of boredom, but they could also be a sign that this person may be tired and not in the best mood to have a conversation.

Emotional - These signals occur when an individual is so overwhelmed with emotions; they can no longer hide it. Crying, crying, looking unhappy, unhappy, sad, visible tremors are some common indicators of emotional body language. It works both ways even with positive emotional body language, and when you're that happy, you can't contain the smile on your face or the leap in your step.

Attentive - These signals become evident when an individual is actively engaged or interested in their surroundings or people. They are focused, pay attention, and maintain good eye contact when they speak. Defensive - Anyone with a strong desire to "protect themselves" will resort to defensive body language. It will be obvious that they are trying to exclude you.

Not all body language gestures have a specific or definitive meaning attached to it. Body language is ambiguous. Depending on the context, it could have different meanings associated with it. The simplest example to illustrate this point is arms crossed in front of the chest gesture, a move that most people do at least once, if not several times a day. It doesn't mean with absolute certainty that you are on the defensive. Not at all. It could mean that you are feeling cold, tired or it could simply mean that you feel this position is the most comfortable for you, which is why you subconsciously do it without even thinking twice. But if you were to do this in front of someone who believes that body language gestures and movements mean very specific things,

Looking for clues on the face

The face is the most moving part of your body, and it's a good place to start looking for clues to see what hidden messages may be masked or hidden through not-so-subtle indicators. Our faces show the strongest emotions, even when you do your best to hide them. Practice your poker face as much as you can, when you feel strong emotions, the briefest glimpse of what is happening below the surface will appear on your face. The naked eye may miss these tiny little gestures, but do it in front of a high-speed camera and even a split-second slip in your poker face will be detected.

This phenomenon of suddenly "leaking" your true emotions, escaping the poker mask you wore to the rest of the world, is known as micro-expressions. They are usually very short and fleeting, sometimes only lasting a fraction of a second. But for those focused on body language analysis, a split second is all they need. FACS is used to perform several functions, which include describing, measuring and interpreting an individual's mannerisms and facial behaviors. In 1970, Paul Ekman and WV Friesen developed what is known as the Facial Action Coding System, or FACS for short. FACS was designed to detect even the smallest contractions and movements of the facial muscles. It then takes the data and determines which category best fits the facial action it detected. FACS, of course, can catch the micro-expressions that appear for the briefest moment on your face, and this makes it a useful device for anyone researching human behavior. Law enforcement agencies rely on FACS to get the truth.

The first clue to look for when analyzing body language is a smile. Generally speaking, there are five types of common smile variations you should look out for:

The Puckered Smile - Lips that are stretched tightly across a person's face to the point where it becomes a straight line while keeping the teeth hidden is known as a puckered smile. A good guess as to what's going on when you see this smile is that the person is trying to hide their annoyance, perhaps. But it could also contain other meanings. It could imply that the person is trying to hold something back. Hiding a secret or fighting the urge to express their opinion, perhaps because they know it may not be appropriate. This smile can also often be seen on women who are too polite to let someone know they might not be interested. Smile sideways while looking up - The person would have their head turned down and turned away while simultaneously looking up at the same time with a tight-lipped smile. It is a sign that the person may be reserved, shy or playful. You may recognize this smile as a favorite of the late Princess Diana, who was often photographed smiling to the side as she looked up. Men are caught when women perform this smile because it evokes their feelings of wanting to protect and care for women.

The Bush Grin - As in George Bush, and there is a reason this category of the smile is named after the former president. Because he seemed to have a smirk on his face that was almost permanent. A permanent smirk gives the impression that you are smug, arrogant, feel superior, or believe you are better than anyone else.

Twisted Smile - Did you know that you could show two opposite emotions on either side of your face? At the same time? The crooked smile or grin is something you may have encountered before. This type of smile often appears when an individual is sarcastic during an argument or debate.

This smile can often be perceived as obnoxious.

What it looks like is the right side of your brain, which is responsible for lifting your left eyebrows, left cheek, and left zygomatic muscles. This causes the right side of your face to be pulled up in a half smile. Now, while the right brain is doing this, the left brain is working to do the opposite. The left side of your brain does all the same things that the right side does, but pulls it down instead. Depending on the context, this smile very often represents sarcasm, because this smile is done more deliberately and is a naturally occurring reaction.

Open-mouthed smile - This smile often reflects that the person is playful or shy. In this case, a person simply lowers their jaw (as the name suggests) to give the playful impression. Like the twisted smile, this is practiced and deliberate.

If someone is avoiding eye contact, there is a strong possibility that they are uncomfortable, uninterested, nervous or bored. Looking someone straight in the eye is almost like looking deep into their soul. Who knew that the eyes could hold so much meaning and clues about it from body language? For example: if their pupils are dilated, it is sure that they are comfortable, maybe even like you. If they blink too unnaturally, there's a strong possibility they may not be entirely honest with you.

If they look to the left, they might recall an authentic memory. If they look to the right, it could be a sign that they are trying to come up with something.

Clues on the jaw

Always staying within the facial area, the next area to focus on in the overall body language analysis is the jaw. Next time you talk to someone, take a quick look at their jaw. Is it tight? Or relaxed? If you notice that your neck muscles may be a little tense, they are giving off signs that they are experiencing a significant amount of discomfort. They may subconsciously signal that they don't want to be a part of this conversation. Or that they may feel tense and stressed about something on their minds.

Head tilted

If you observe that the person you are conversing with tilts their head slightly when you speak, it is their body's way of letting you know that they are interested, trust you and approve of you. It means there is a relationship going on there. Former President Barack Obama, during some of his political debates, often tilted his head to the side, indicating that he understood where his political opponents came from.

Arms folded

As we have already established, having your arms crossed over your chest could mean many different things. Bending one or both arms across our bodies is our subconscious way of forming a "protective barrier" to protect us from perceived threats or undesirable situations. It could be a sign that someone is feeling nervous, anxious, defensive, angry, impatient, or perhaps none of the above, and they may just find this position natural and comfortable.

While it is a common gesture, it is also a daunting gesture due to the apparent signal that you either don't want to be involved or you don't want to participate. It makes the one who takes this position seem unapproachable. Some people do it because they feel comfortable, while others do it because on the inside they feel negatively about the person or situation. Both arms crossed directly across the chest are often perceived as less than welcoming and may discourage others because they assume you are angry or closed to them or your situation.

Clues about hand gestures

Hand gestures offer an intriguing insight into a person's innermost thoughts and emotions. Hand gestures are as much a part of our communication process as our words. When used correctly, the gesture causes people to notice what you are trying to say, especially when you correctly accompany those gestures with the words you are trying to emphasize. Hand gestures are in abundance and some of the common meanings associated with familiar gestures include the following:

Rub your eyes - Tiredness or fatigue.

Scrub the eyebrows - Worried or doubtful.

Ear rubbing: Rubbing behind the ears is an indication that the person is afraid of being misunderstood or does not understand.

Earlobe Touch - Maybe looking for comfort.

Running your fingers through your hair - Unsure, unsure or trying to think.

Head Scratch - Deep thought or confusion (depending on the context).

I am stroking my chin - thinking of something.

Index finger on the temple - Also, an indication that the person is thinking about something or is deep in their thoughts.

Nose Touch - Lying or feeling pressured.

Arms outstretched, palms open - an indication of the person's openness.

Pointing the finger - An indication that a person feels authoritative.

Sometimes, this could be an indication of aggressive or angry emotions. Open Palms - An indication of honesty and a way of subconsciously saying they are not a threat.

Pointed feet

If someone likes you and is comfortable with you, you will notice that their toes are pointing inward and pointing in your direction. But of course there is more at our feet than meets the eye. Some of the more common leg movement gestures include:

Standing crossed legs - an indication that a person may be feeling shy. It can be seen as a submissive position or a sign that a person is not completely comfortable with their surroundings or the person they are talking to.

Sitting down, legs slightly apart - an indication that the person feels both relaxed and comfortable.

Crossed Legs While Sitting, Relax: If this gesture is accompanied by the person crossing their arms over their chest, it can be an indication that they are emotionally withdrawn or closed.

Sitting, crossed ankles: signals that the person is feeling relaxed. When accompanied by clenched hands, it could be an indication that the person is feeling stiff or tense, or a signal of self-control.

Can you pretend until you do it?

To some extent, we have control over the gestures we choose to exhibit when we consciously choose to do so. During a speech, for example, or when you requisition a meeting. You can choose the way you project yourself, the hand gestures you want to do, the position you want to assume while speaking. Sometimes you may want to hide your sincere feelings. Or even what you might think. We don't want everyone else to know what's going on inside. In that sense, yes, we can pretend to some extent. But at the end of the day, our bodies have a mind of their own. No matter how hard we try to hide it or consciously control it, your body will still give small signs and signals that the message you are conveying may not be entirely accurate. To an inexperienced eye, you may be able to pass that all is well. Those who know what to look for can spot signs that may not be all as it seems. As long as body language exists, the lies and inconsistencies in the story being told will eventually be revealed. Always.

Chapter 5: verbal vs non-verbal

The language is amazing. As humans, we have an incredible ability to communicate with each other. This level of communication is part of the reason why we have been able to advance so far in our evolution. The progress of our communication translates into progress in our society. In this chapter, we will discuss the ways in which our communication is more advanced and the complexities behind verbal and non-verbal behavior. More importantly, we will define non-verbal and verbal behavior and also provide two differences between the two and learn how to analyze the statements that other individuals make verbally. More specifically, we will learn how to analyze these verbal statements using non-verbal language. We will also enter into the complexity of

Definition of non-verbal behavior

Non-verbal behavior or communication is the subconscious or conscious transmission of ideas or emotions through physical movement or a series of well-known and understood gestures. Messages can be transferred non-verbally through a variety of signals and methods.

The first of these defining cues are methods known as proxemics. Proxemics essentially means the distance between two individuals. The distance between two individuals or proxemics has a lot of weight in terms of non-verbal communication.

The second method of non-verbal communication is known as kinetics and is simply another word for body language. Kinesics or body language is the transmission of ideas through often unconscious gestures and movements of the body.

Meanwhile, another method of definition is known as haptic. Haptics is another word for the act of touching something. In the world of non-verbal behavior, how someone touches something carries a lot of weight in communicating their emotions to another individual. A soft touch on the arm can mean many things, which become very different than a firm grip on your hand. Not all touches are the same and each touch, depending on its longevity, intensity and position on the body, has many different meanings behind it.

Another form of non-verbal communication is our appearance. People use their looks to communicate their personality in various ways. Most of this is a conscious decision made by the individual, but there are some factors almost entirely caused by our parents that are not necessarily chosen by us but still say things about ourselves. Most likely, the largest and most common type of non-verbal communication with our parents is simply judging whether or not someone cares about their appearance. By simply looking at another person, we can immediately tell whether or not they care about how they appear to those around them. This carries a tremendous amount of weight in the quick judgment we give people every single day. L' The last common form of non-verbal communication is the use of eye contact. Eye contact is extremely important to us humans. Human beings are very focused on an individual's eyes, as this is often one of the first things a person looks at when seeing a new face. Your eyes are often considered the windows to the soul, and this is true in the sense that they can reveal many factors about you. By looking someone in the eye or measuring the amount of eye contact they give, we can understand a great deal of information about their personality. Do they have strong eye contact? Do they avoid eye contact? Do they have really intense eye contact? The answers to all these questions give us different definitions of a person's personality. As human beings,

Verbal communication seems fairly obvious when it is spoken aloud. Verbal communication obviously consists of any form of speech or language used to convey ideas or thoughts to another. Verbal communication includes much more than just talking to a person. The way we combine ideas and thoughts with words shows much of their personality in the words we choose in the cadence we choose to put them together. There are many ways we can express ourselves through verbal communication. The first and most obvious way we can express ourselves through verbal communication is to speak to those around us. By putting words and phrases together, we create coherent thoughts and ideas that express our feelings to those around us.

In addition to being able to accurately and positively express our emotions and feelings to those around us, the act of speaking is also easy enough to use to persuade or alter our true meaning. It is much easier to verbally lie to a person than to lie to a person with our body language. For this reason, we often find people who lie very easily by voice, but whose body language signals do not match their words.

The second form of verbal communication, writing, may come as a surprise to some people who read this text. The act of writing, while not technically verbal, still includes verbal communication because it uses common spoken language simply in written form. The difficulty with this is that a person reading a text has much more difficulty guessing and understanding the cadence than the person who wrote the text. Because of this, written ideas and emotions can be misinterpreted due to the fact that people are unable to fully tell the intonation of the author of the text through words.

Another form of verbal communication is an underlying feeling within our words known as a denotation or connotation. Connotation is considered to be the feelings or emotions associated with the meanings of certain words or phrases. This is not to be confused with its opposite, denotation, which is the literal or primary meaning of a word, as opposed to the emotions or series the word suggests. To convey these important forms of verbal communication, a person must use our neck verbal form of communication.

The next form of verbal communication we're going to talk about is tone and volume. A person's tone, when talking to another person, can express a lot about that person's inner thoughts or feelings. Tone is a very difficult form of communication to define and explain to people. For some individuals, the tone is very easy to control and change in their language, while for others it can be very difficult. You cannot describe the tone as based on the inflection an individual gives to certain words at certain times. The tone is very interesting because each person is able to understand the meaning behind the tones of others almost in perfect connection with each other, but it is very difficult to explain to others. In relation to this, a person ' The volume is also of great importance in their verbal communication. Since childhood, we have all learned the difference between an internal voice and an external voice. Do the volume levels show much of our emotions? We can read a lot about how someone feels in a given situation based on their volume at that moment.

It is important to always remember that it is necessary to simultaneously use verbal and non-verbal forms of communication to understand the overall result of a person's ideas and theories. A common misconception among individuals is that verbal communication and non-verbal communication are contradictory. This is not the case. Verbal and non-verbal communication must go side by side when communicating with those around us. It is the combination of these two complex forms of communication that makes the translation of our ideas and theories the most effective. One cannot exist without the other in most cases. It is often stated by body language specialists that non-verbal communication can play one of five roles when trying to read another person.

Substitution: Some types of non-verbal communication are initiated as a substitution or placement for verbal communication. Examples of this are nodding your head for yes or shrugging your shoulders for "I don't know".

Reinforcement: Non-verbal communication can often be used to reinforce a previously given statement. By reading an individual's body language and judging it consistently, you can almost completely ascertain whether he is telling the truth or not.

Contradiction: This is the opposite of reinforcement. If a person's body language seems to contradict something they are saying, then under the contradiction rule, they almost certainly lie, depending on their environment, of course.

Accentuation: Body language often serves as a method of accentuating something a person says vocally. Examples of this include smiling when someone says they are happy or shaking when someone says they are cold. This can also be used to give more importance to a claim that someone has made. An example is creating the quotation mark symbol with your fingers while saying something in a sarcastic way. By adding body language to the statement you are making, you are reaffirming and showing importance in your statement.

Regulation: An individual's body can also serve to regulate that person's speech language.

Chapter 6: Emotional Intelligence

No doubt you've heard the term emotional intelligence often. Although it is now commonplace, emotional intelligence has been used extensively from the 1990s to the present, popularized by science journalist Daniel Goleman and backed by the work of several psychologists. The most prominent proponents of this theory were John Mayer and Peter Salovey who, in the late 1990s, published several research papers with working conceptual models based on the concept and supporting it as a counterpoint to the IQ test. The concept has remained popular ever since and has become a key part of the business management approach in many large companies. To explain the concept of emotional intelligence, we will first examine what its basis is.

What is emotional intelligence:

Psychologists have traditionally broken down the mind into cognition, affection, and motivation.

Cognition refers to reasoning, memory and judgment. This aspect of the mind is what most psychologists currently base their intelligence measurements on, such as the famous intelligence quotient (IQ) advocated by William Stern at the University of Wroclaw in his 1912 book "Psychological Methods to Test intelligence ". With the advent of the industrial revolution in the late 18th century, the measure of success a person could hope to achieve was heavily based on his ability to reason, manipulate three-dimensional space and develop new technologies. To gain some kind of insight into this it is enough to look at the folk figures of Victorian-era Britain which include; Isambard Kingdom Brunel, prolific engineer of bridges, ships and architectural wonders; Robert Stevenson, the creator of the steam locomotive and Charles Babbage,

Affection refers to moods, emotions and energy. Someone with strong affection is prone to have strong emotions and feelings than someone with weak affection who appears indifferent to most emotions. Affection is not something that has traditionally been quantifiable, which has made it difficult to study using a quantifiable scientific methodology. This has been partially solved by advances in modern technology, such as CT scans and electroencephalography measurement, and in part by the large increase in scientific articles dealing specifically with this topic. This is relevant at the time of publication in the midst of what is called the replication crisis. This refers to the volume of low-quality research that has been published in multiple social fields, including psychology, which is not repeatable under the same conditions outlined in the initial research. In other words, when other experiments are repeated different results are produced. While this is a topic that can be discussed in depth, for the purposes of this book we will only mention it in regards to emotional intelligence. Part of the solution to such a replication crisis is to use what is called "meta-analysis" of documents. Simply put, this means taking a large subset of the current literature and grouping it together, taking an average, as it were, of the results. Several independent meta-analysis studies have shown that the emotional intelligence is a significant factor in improving mental and physical health. for the purposes of this book we will only mention it in regards to emotional intelligence. Part of the solution to such a replication crisis is to use what is called "meta-analysis" of documents. Simply put, this means taking a large subset of the current literature and grouping it together, taking an average, as it were, of the results. Several independent meta-analysis studies have shown that emotional intelligence is a significant factor in improving mental and physical health. for the purposes of this book we will only mention it in respect of emotional intelligence. Part of the solution to such a replication crisis is to use what is called "meta-analysis" of documents. Simply put, this means taking a large subset of the current literature and grouping it together, taking an average, as it were, of the results. Several independent meta-analysis studies have shown that emotional intelligence is a significant factor in improving mental and physical health.

Motivation refers to the ability to initiate, lead and maintain oneself in relation to goals. These are divided into extrinsic motivations, such as those that occur externally to an individual, and intrinsic motivations, which occur within oneself. For the purpose of this book we will examine the most commonly used theory: Maslow's hierarchy of needs. Developed in the mid-1950s, Abraham Maslow hypothesized that a person has specific needs that must be met in order to rise to the next level of satisfaction or motivation. These include; basic physiological needs (hunger, thirst, sleep, etc.); a safe home; social needs; recognition and possibly self-actualization (full potential for realization).

The combination of cognition and affection leads to what is called emotional intelligence. Note that this is a general statement that the combination of the two is not always related to this.

To summarize: emotional intelligence refers to a person's ability to; identify and name one's emotions, use emotions to apply them and manage one's own and others' emotions.

How to improve your emotional intelligence:

Now that we have a background on what emotional intelligence means, let's see how we can improve ours.

We've already partially covered identifying and naming your emotions in a basic way earlier in the book, so in this part of the book we'll cover how to harness emotions and apply the insights from them to help yourself and others.

To understand what people think, or predict what people might feel, we must first learn what kinds of feelings exist most frequently for humans. Human beings have one of the most complex thought systems known in the animal kingdom. The first step towards emotional intelligence is to accept your emotions. You can't start helping others with your emotions if you don't accept and acknowledge your own. Personalities are formed in early childhood, which means that it is very difficult to effectively change your intrinsic emotional reactions to internal and external stimuli.

Before trying to emotionally interact with others, consider your reactions and that someone may not react the same way as you. It can and will be easy to simply assume a "fact" about someone in general before you have any kind of valid evidence to back up your feelings about him. Seeing a person act condescendingly towards others could trigger an unconscious memory of a bully from your childhood that you may project onto them, even if the person doesn't share other traits. You can see someone doing something like biking or eating vegan foods without thinking twice, but you always have to find your base first. The search for evidence begins immediately. For a person to tell if they find someone attractive, it takes less than 2 seconds. This first impression takes less than 2 seconds. Start by finding a base.

Let's take an example. Let's say you just met a colleague who drove you to a restaurant on a lunch break at work.

Remarks:
1. I see an open can of alcohol in their car
2. It's 1pm on Thursday
3. (Inferred knowledge) Alcoholics often drink at unsociable hours of the day

Assumption:

1. I think this person is an alcoholic because I can see open bottles of drinks in their car and they are drinking at 1am
2. My father drank a lot many times throughout the day and was an alcoholic, so this person is an alcoholic

If you can, take note of your personal assumptions, such as hypothesis 2, and try to see if this is helpful in this situation. In order to understand them emotionally, ask yourself why you think they are doing this before going deeper.

Hypothesis:

1. They are drinking as a means of distracting themselves from a problem
2. They don't properly manage their emotional problems
3. They may have a long-term problem with drinking

Try to get more information about this person to see if this supports your assumptions and assumptions. Ask them or others about these particular observations. Take care of how you do it, remember to be humble and non-invasive. On this occasion it can be revealed that their mother died earlier that day and, to numb the pain, your co-worker is drowning their pains. Alternatively, you may not be able to get a response from your co-worker and, after a couple of weeks, you notice that this behavior hasn't recurred and they are always sober.

Perhaps the most important part of this process is keeping the variables constant. The empirical approach, as introduced in chapter 2, is useful for all forms of scientific observation and are useful for studying others. To recap, the following steps are essential:

1. Make observations
2. Make assumptions based on your observations
3. Find a way to test your hypotheses

4. Accept or reject your assumptions
5. Use this information

Each time, obey this process. If you do the same thing every time, you get much more accurate results than changing your methodology. As martial artist Bruce Lee once said, "I'm not afraid of the man who kicked 10,000 times once, but I fear the man who kicked 10,000 times." Let's look at the steps in more detail.

Look closely at a person's body language, tone of voice, behavior, and previous behaviors. The more observations you make, the better your inferences and assumptions will be. Don't forget to use your intuition, as outlined in Chapter 4, as a tool to help you get more information and to model your assumptions.

Secondly, make your first impression. This is your guess. Do you think they are someone you could be friends with or do you have reservations about them? However, don't make it a heavy or permanent label. This is just a guess and has little value without testing. It would be inappropriate for you to say what you have heard about others before you know them well enough.

Third, your hypothesis is verified. Ask them questions about themselves, they may be someone more like you than you think. See if they constantly exhibit these behaviors. The consistency of a person's actions will tell you whether your first impressions are correct or not.

Fourth, embrace your findings. It may surprise you to learn that this person is different from what you supposed, or on the contrary, you may be completely correct.

Regardless of your conclusion, remain open to the possibility that this person could change for better or for worse. People can change, and that's okay, especially when you're young.

Using emotional intelligence to deal with deceptive individuals:

Now for a practical example of using emotional intelligence to find deceptive individuals. These could be manipulators, liars, or potential B group personalities.

Everyone lies:

It's the classic quote from the late 2000s medical / investigative drama House MD but, while we're not emotionally complex doctors with Vicodin habits, this is very true. Researcher Bella DePaula conducted research in the late 1990s showing that, during self-report, college students who were part of the study tended to tell 2 lies a day. Most of these were self-centered lies, as opposed to other-oriented lies.

Some lies are commonly told to protect us and our feelings from being harmed. These lies are known as white lies, said to save someone's feelings. Tell someone that they look good in their new clothes, when you actually think it doesn't suit them. When you tell someone how much you like their new car when they reveal it, even if you specifically would never buy it, they are both examples of white lies. Buckling or spreading the truth to make someone feel better or to spare their feelings is a lie that is said not to hurt anyone who hears it. We tell these lies almost every day and these white lies typically save a lot of broken feelings and wrong statements. While these lies are obviously not harmful and often cannot be detected, DePaula 'Research clearly showed that people who lied in this way often reported their less pleasant and less intimate conversations. Remember this when you decide to tell a white lie yourself. Lies bigger than white lies, however, can harm many people, and these are the kinds of lies we can teach to notice. We'll take a look at some of the main clues to lying below.

Contradiction:

We need to be aware of ourselves. Nobody likes to be lied to, and hopefully if you're using the analytical techniques found in this book, you can observe the people around you and see if their behavior is sincere.

We've already talked about body language and the idea that someone's actions should match the words they're talking about. The old saying, "actions speak louder than words" is pretty good, but there are other tools you can use to gauge whether the person you're looking at is wary. A great indication that someone is lying is if they are telling contradictory stories. If someone tells a story once and then tells it again in front of another crowd and the details change, it is likely that all or part of the story is made up or embellished enough to make it completely false. Someone might do this to avoid getting into trouble if the story makes them seem unfavorable, or to make them seem more interesting if they are trying to impress someone.

Consistency:

Those who lie often often find it difficult to remember their previous lies. Liars often have a hard time distinguishing their lies from their truths and as a result, they weave multiple stories that push them further into a web of lies. Another explanation for why the story might change, or at least show some contradictions, is that the person doesn't know why they lied to begin with. Think of a teenager who lies to avoid getting into trouble. He or she may tell a parent that they spent the night at a friend's house, but when they retell the story to the other parent, they will give another friend or another name whose home they visited during the night. As the parents compare the notes, they catch their child in a lie because the child doesn't remember enough details to keep the same story, or they haven't planned their stories in detail. Small details may be enough to reveal the plot.

Perfect responses and stall:

A great indicator that someone is lying is if they have an answer to something, even if the situation requires them to think about the answer first. DePaula coined the term "Deliberateness" to describe these kinds of people in the studios who were not acting naturally but were almost playing a role they had written for themselves. Someone who has a ready answer has most likely already thought about what they will say and the story they intend to weave. If the question you ask will require some kind of thought memory or some sort of wording of the answer, but the person can just give the answer without any thought, they may be lying.

Questions, especially questions involving a recollection of memories or an interpretation of feelings, cannot always be answered without a thought in the answers. If someone gives you a short answer and responds too quickly, they may be lying.

A significant sign that someone is playing on time is when your question is answered. If you ask someone a basic question and they hesitate to answer or repeat the question to "ask for clarification", they may be lying. A liar will try to buy more time to find a plausible excuse for the question you asked, or they will try to avoid answering the question completely.

Wrong direction:

In addition to repeating your questions, one of the strategies a liar can use to divert your attention or try to distract you from not wanting to answer your question is to answer your question with a question. If you ask others for a specific action or a reason to do something, they will always try to divert your attention by challenging you. For example, if you think your spouse or significant other is cheating on you or lying about their whereabouts, you might ask, "Where were you last night? I tried to call you." Instead of apologizing to you and instead of asking you where they were the night before, they may answer your question with a similar one. "Where have you been? Why do you want to contact me?". By returning your attention to yourself, they divert the attention from your questions and try to make you feel that they should be as concerned as you are, even when they know they are wrong. In a way, by answering your questions with questions of their own, a liar can change the subject or shorten their story. Clearly, someone who is lying has something to hide. Whether it's something they're ashamed of or something they have trouble with, their main focus is on focusing on something else. By answering your questions in a word or two, and then shifting your attention to another topic, they can divert attention from themselves and talk about something else. This quick change of subject is also used as a joke in movies and sitcoms when a character asks another character a question, and the character replies, "

Emotional mismatch:

Some people who lie distort their faces to create more exaggerated and deceptive facial expressions. They might do this to make their story more persuasive when it actually has the opposite effect. Look for excessive gestures that seem unnecessarily dramatic or gestures that don't fit the emotions of the plot, such as someone making an overly frowning expression when telling a story. Something that supposedly drove the narrator crazy might not arouse anger, something that supposedly deeply upset him can be explained in extreme logical detail.

Police frequently interrogate witnesses in criminal cases and find they lie, not just because of the contradictory claims they may make, but because they don't show the appropriate emotions. Anyone who has just lost a family member to murder could lie about parts or the whole thing if they can't express the right feelings they would have after losing someone. Anyone who is lying may even stop thinking about themselves. The bad child will often refrain from using the word "I" in their stories. Avoiding the use of first-person words is a psychological method used by liars to shift attention and get away from the situation or embellish their story. By avoiding the use of first-person terms, the liar can distance himself from the story, making the lies less serious. Imagine this scenario: You're making plans with a friend you don't want to see. Your friend is excited about the plans and you don't want to cancel them, even if you fear the case. If you tell your friend "I'm looking forward to tomorrow", you walk away from the event by avoiding using language in the first person. Which of these phrases is more sincere: "Don't wait until tomorrow!" Or "Can't wait until tomorrow!

"? The last sentence, the second sentence, the use

of the" I "in the first person sounds more sincere.

Presentation:

Our second practical example for this section is the presentation. We define presentation as how people want to withdraw and reflect themselves in the outside world. How someone introduces themselves can be the key to understanding how they feel and how they treat them.

Observe the initial, superficial, outward appearance of an individual. Are they wearing a sporty suit and elegant, comfortable shoes that reflect ambition? Jeans and a T-shirt that shows warmth and ease? A dress with a wide neckline, a seductive choice? A crucifix or a Buddha, which suggests spiritual values?

We will start by thinking about modest beliefs. Modest clothing is an illustration of a presentation, so I'll clarify how it should relate and what kind of person it is. Clinical psychologist Dr. Jennifer Baumgartner has studied this in detail by looking at what she calls "fashion psychology." He argues that, because our bodies don't always immediately show what social or socioeconomic class we are, humans depend on clothing, jewelry, and accessories to increase their value. People dress according to the income they get. People in today's society feel that their value is tremendously determined by how much money they make and how much they own. We live in a material and contemporary world. Ordinary people want to blend in with social groups. It is not uncommon for a child to turn 9 or 10 and start asking for specific clothes at Christmas and birthdays. You want to connect with your friends and wear the same clothes and especially the same brands as your popular friends.

This continues into adulthood as well. Sometimes people with low self-esteem, who rely on social media, spend an excessive or even unreasonable amount on clothes with a brand. This is similar to someone visiting Starbucks instead of the gas station because they want to be seen there and not because they like coffee more. For some people, this is a huge challenge and a convenient pit to slip into. You can definitely assume that anyone you meet similar to this will face difficulties like low self-esteem, low sense of trust and isolation because they are constantly trying to look like their famous idols or have more friends by getting more "likes" on social media. You will also meet people in your life who prefer to dress very well.

One thing to note is the lack of attention to clothing that depressed people can display. Depression sometimes manifests itself in forms that not only physically but also psychologically affect individuals. A depressed person loses the will to take care of himself. Common physical manifestations of depression include neglecting one's appearance, including not washing one's hair, ignoring oral hygiene, wearing dirty or stubborn clothes, or outrageously bad clothes. Sometimes, even if it doesn't fit, people choose to keep their clothes on for a long time. They wear old pairs of socks, hoodies and t-shirts from their exes and pants they haven't been able to wear in years. These people can stay true to their past. Those clothes can bring back memories of these people, like when you see people wearing band shirts, reminding them of the concerts they've been to in the past. These people might still enjoy life and keeping memories of good times is a lesson for all of us to make sure that before it's too late, we enjoy life.

Pay attention to how your clothes fit your body. Sometimes people with body dysmorphism or problems with their appearance wear clothes that are too large. They do this to feel safer or more comfortable rather than revealing their bodies to others. It is not uncommon to see people who associate or have low self-esteem with introverts. When people feel comfortable and enjoy their body, they wear clothes that fit them. It is a symbol of a person who feels confident in himself.

Another indicator for people with self-esteem issues is that they wear dark, dull, colorless, and neutral clothing. The main goal is not to draw attention to themselves, so that they are not stared wherever they go. If people with high self-esteem go out for the evening, there is no difficulty in wearing a shiny and colorful Hawaiian floral shirt with white shorts. They like to talk through their clothes, and that's okay! Those who choose to wear calmer tones can express themselves with other things such as art or music. Neutral tones can also be a sign of someone trying to dress up or look mature and professional. In the closet, color isn't everything, so obviously it doesn't keep everyone away! When you are around observe the way others dress and the way they want to show themselves and take note. This is the first thing you see and it will play an important role in your decision making. Note, clothes aren't everything, but they play an important role.

The general appearance comes in other forms besides clothing, such as in personal care, so pay attention and you will be able to determine the characteristics of those around you.

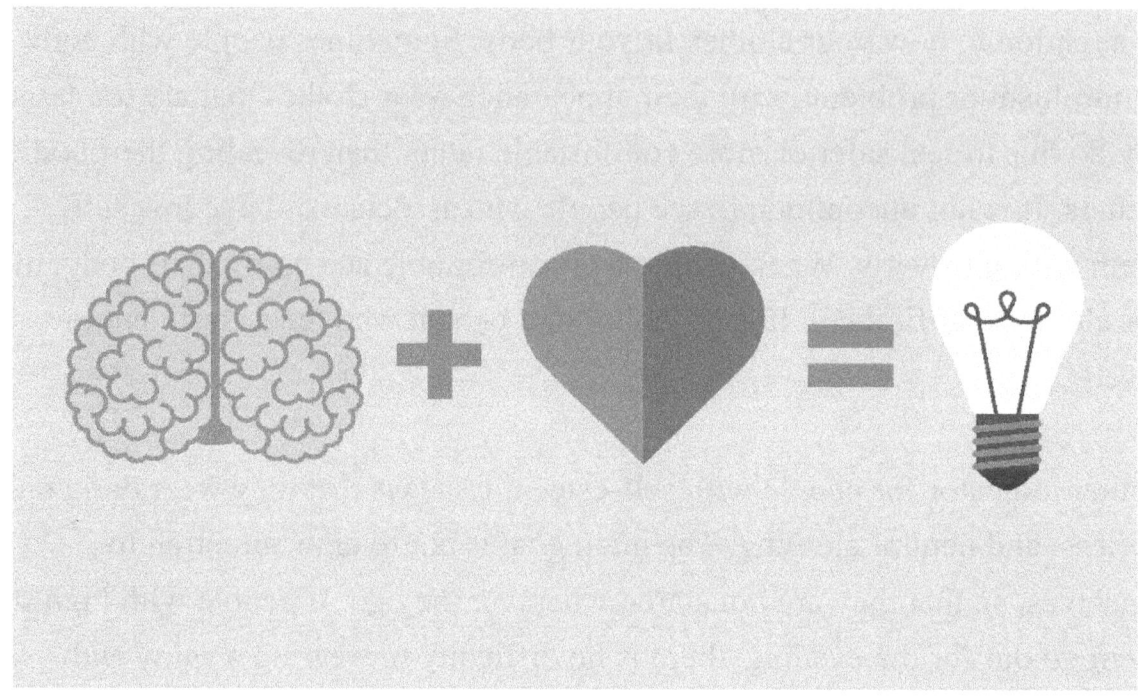

Chapter 7: Personality

Every day you may encounter new personality types, some close to our characteristics and others completely new. Although no two personalities are alike, some personality forms are comparable and can be generalized. This is what we mean by personality type. Although the focus of this book is on analyzing people on a more personal and practical level (microanalysis), we have included this chapter for those interested in the broader study of personality types to help identify broader trends (macro analysis). The history of grouping people according to personality has a long and complex history, dating back at least to the ancient Pergamonian, Galen, which is the theory of the four temperaments, built on even older Hippocratic beliefs in his dissertation De temperamentis between AD 165 and 175 Great thinkers from Paracelsus to Kant developed similar theories based on the four temperament model before a scientific focus was applied to the question in the 20th century. These included:

Bloodthirsty individuals who were outgoing, sociable, and outgoing

Extroverted, dominant and assertive choleric individuals

Melancholy individuals who were introverted, analytical and perfectionists

Phlegmatic individuals who were introverted, relaxed and accommodating

The rise of industrialized industry and new management techniques have led to the desire for personality testing, a way to accurately assess another person's temperament in order to ensure their suitability for work and for managers to manage themselves with greater ease. The 1919 Woodworth Psychoneurotic Inventory was originally developed to be used in the screening of bullet shock victims for the US military, but has been extensively adapted to be used as the basis of many modern personality tests.

As the century went by, the main personality test turned to the five-factor model, introduced in the early 1960s by Ernest Tupes and Raymond Christal but popularized in the scientific community in the late 1980s by JM Digman and

Lewis Goldman who both expanded the model with their own thoughts. Characteristics measured by the five-factor model include:

Openness to experience: how willing a person is to new experiences
Conscientiousness: how willing a person is to complete responsible tasks and actions
Extroversion: How willing a person is to socialize with others
Agreeableness: how willing a person is to accept current situations and individuals
Neuroticism: how willing a person is to tolerate situations

Personality types are essentially human personality models, and as with all models, you shouldn't take them as pure facts, simply as tools to help make large-scale observations of generalized personality types. As with any field that delves into managing large datasets, there will always be fringe cases and data that doesn't fit your theory / model. Contrary to this, it is also necessary to understand that the creation of these large-scale models can bring benefits to research or large-scale organizations that cannot be described by small-scale phenomena.

Since personality types are based on general traits and responses, they don't describe every single human personality in the world. It is important to note that people can have specific personality characteristics, but also be identified as having a different personality type. Specific tests are performed to classify a person's personality type, and each person's particular type is determined based on the decisions made by each respondent. The assignment is based on the group closest to the test subject's answers.

In this chapter we will mainly examine the theory of personality types A and B, such as; an example of the positive and negative aspects of personality theories and tests; to give you guidance on how to deal with these two types based on the assumption that they are correct and act as a warning to address personality theories and apply your logical faculties, set out in previous chapters, to scientific research.

Origins:

This personality theory was created in the 1950s by two cardiologists, Howard Friedman and Ray Rosenman, who mainly focused on determining the likelihood that personality had in developing heart disease. Their primary focus was to determine which personality traits led to coronary heart disease, a huge 20th century medical problem that resulted in significant deaths in the United States during this time.

Type A personality:

Those with a type A temperament are generally known to be more motivated and more likely to achieve their goals. type A is usually creative, inspired and disciplined. They stick to a strict schedule and don't want to deviate from the norm. Type A temperament thrives on feeling accomplished and loves making lists, taking something off the path and then moving fast. Type A temperament also requires several activities and finds leisure or free time a waste of energy. You find it difficult to remain inactive, as you would like to finish one mission and move on to the next. Type A temperament also has little or no tolerance with others for doing wrong work. Instead of taking time out of the day to delegate the position to another person, they prefer to take care of certain tasks themselves. Not only do they have tolerance issues, but they still have trouble expressing concern for others and are often immediately frustrated. Type A is usually an overachiever and a workaholic, sometimes spending more energy and resources on their work and profession than on their family or relationships. Type A is always on the go, talks fast, drives fast, and acts desperate. These traits are typically associated with other stress-related problems, including stroke, high blood pressure, or heart pain. Type A traits are now so distinct that it is now popular to name anyone "type A" if guided and controllable behavior occurs. Although Type A attitude is usually pessimistic, individuals exhibiting certain behavioral traits are the "agents" of the planet. They organize activities, plan excursions, and conduct meetings. Despite the type A people of the world, little will ever be done. Temperament in category B is at the opposite end of the continuum. Although there is a lot of research and knowledge on the Type A personality, the Type B personality is mostly classified simply as "someone else".

Type B personality:

Someone identified as a type B individual is typically calmer and easier to manage. They are not easily disturbed and typically exhibit a more fluid attitude. Rather than actively handling the case, the characteristics of Type B seem to be able to respond more and more to situations. Category B personalities are always casual and pleasant, and the two personality forms are more sociable and / or likeable. Type B personalities like to work in the community and don't get angry quickly. The temperament of type B is, therefore, much more intense and reproducible. Regardless of their feelings and uncertainties, they also find it difficult to make choices and stay true to their decisions. Therefore, the temperament of category B continues to be capricious.

It is difficult for the type B person to worry about the future and is generally not afraid of what the future holds. The type B temperament makes them a strong companion as they are more relaxed and less aggressive overall. Someone who exhibits type B traits is less prone to experiencing traumatic diseases, such as stroke, high blood pressure, and heart failure. Type B temperament operates intensely but at a particular pace. Type B people are more prone to take risks and struggle to see their mistakes as an opportunity to learn. Once the Type B personality completes a task or milestone, it takes time to celebrate its success before moving on to the next project. They enjoy their free time and need time to relax.

Comparison:

For Type A personalities, those who display Type B traits can be considered indecisive and difficult to manage; the type B font, on the other hand, makes things fun and carefree. Type B is the group dreamer, who thinks and runs on elaborate ideas.

We have described how the Type A temperament is set, time-bound and always in motion. For someone who wants to take their time completing assignments and making decisions, the Type A temperament is found a little more overwhelming. However, the combination of the two types offers easy solutions. When you are not a Type A personality, you should first be on time to relieve anxiety. Type A people do not like to waste time, and if they have to sit and wait, they will feel like they are wasting time and spending time doing something productive. Don't needlessly chat with a Type A personality. Just like you don't want to hesitate, you don't want to waste time chatting with others or listening to someone who has a complicated lie. Go to the point, tell what you have to say and provide relevant information, but don't include detailed, unnecessary details. Stick to a time limit.

For a type A, even if a project is finished, you have to move on to the next thing and move on. When form A's temperament is anxious, focus on activities that calm him down. Disabling situations you realize would make them angry. For starters, if someone you meet has a Type A personality, make sure the overhead projector works when they arrive at the workplace. Nothing will make a Type A personality more angry than wasting time on things they think could have been worked out before they arrived. You would definitely feel like you are spending your precious time trying to fix the problem. Many people known to be Type A personalities often don't know they are unreasonably angry. You can help a type

A, telling him to relax in a situation (and help him get along with a type B). In particular, don '

An individual with a Type B personality may seem casual to a Type A personality, even if they don't intend to be. Their cheeky Type A essence is part of who they are, so they often don't even know they're being rude or cold. They are on a mission and can only see what leads to their goal. Type A temperament is that of a person who is constantly alert and running. It all may seem like a struggle to them from a stranger's point of view. Don't try to turn everything into a competition if you want to get along with someone who is Type A. Recognize that their hardworking demeanor and motivated personality can in many ways be positive and let go. If you are married or related to someone who has a Type A personality, let them know that you ' Not attempting to compete or beat them in any category often makes them less aggressive and allows them to relax a little. Those people with strong Type A personalities often try, even when not necessary, to compete. Trying not to compete with them all the time, you let them know that they have some freedom to relax with you. Set limitations for interacting with A types. We've already mentioned why someone who exhibits these characteristics sometimes struggles to grasp the approach of someone who doesn't have the same characteristics. Sometimes they are not meant to make people feel small. By making them understand that their behavior is discouraging and unacceptable, you can make them aware of how their actions impact others. They probably have no idea how you feel and the feedback will help them grow as a person. Just as some find it difficult to cope with Type A personalities, Type B personalities can cause difficulties for others. Some B-types are inclined to be dreamers, investing time to see the bigger picture and enjoy their results. Type A might consider it a waste of time, but Type B needs to recharge and take much-needed breaks. B-types need this break and they won't work well, with small details when stressed. You can allow B-types to thrive with imaginative ideas and creative work goals, but don't underline them with minute details. They don't want things to fall into an exact box and always work fine when you have the opportunity to be innovative and create your own solutions. Although Type B's temperament is always softer and more carefree, he notes that he is still individual. So, even though this individual may not be bound, they still have specific things that are important in their life just like everyone else. Allow them to feel frustrated if something goes wrong and to know they have strong emotions. Even if they don't rush to communicate, their time is as precious as anyone else, so if you dump them or wait too long, they'll probably get mad like any type A. Type B temper is well rounded, partly because they're so straightforward. and they are met by most people. They are perfect for being exposed to many companies and prospects and having them around adds a great deal of information to the table. Allow them to feel frustrated if something goes wrong and to know they have strong emotions. Even if they don't rush to communicate, their time is as precious as anyone else, so if you dump them or wait too long, they'll probably get mad like any type A. Type B temper is well rounded, partly because they're so straightforward. and they are met by most people. They are perfect for being exposed to many companies and prospects, and having them around adds a great deal of information to the table. Allow them to feel frustrated if something goes wrong and to know they have strong emotions. Even if they don't rush to communicate, their time is as precious as anyone else, so if you dump them or wait too long, they will probably get mad like any type A. Type B temperament is well rounded, partly because they are so straightforward and are met by most people . They are perfect for being exposed to many companies and prospects, and having them around adds a great deal of information to the table.

Rating:

So after reading the above, what can you discern between Type A and Type B personalities? The above advice for dealing with these personalities is quite valid, based on the observation that these two types exist. Based on the two personality descriptions you can create a logical framework that you can use to give practical advice, as outlined above. There is only one problem though: we hypothesized that the two personality types exist and have been observed.

Let's dig a little deeper with some evidence-based research papers to corroborate this theory. A 1987 study at the University of California found that, in fact, counseling for type A personalities helped reduce the incidence of coronary heart disease to a statistically significant level compared to a control group. Basically, confirming the theory. Other studies performed from the late 1960s to early 1990s also match such as the Western Collaborative Group Study and the Framingham Study. Unfortunately, it so happened that several major studies supporting the theory were significantly funded by the tobacco industry which was found to have influenced some of the main research findings. Whether it was selling cigarettes to relax Type A personalities or to shift the blame for deaths from coronary heart disease this throws a dark light on the validity of the theory. However, there are still some studies that support this theory, but the model has become obscure and out of the public eye.

As pointed out in the introduction to this chapter, the most popular current model for testing personality is the five-factor model. In contrast to the personality theory of type A and type B, this was developed by multiple individual psychological researchers in the late 20th century and is based on psychological factors rather than factors that contribute to cardiological disease and the risk of coronary heart disease. . Variants of this model are commonly used today and its foundations have been found reasonably solid. Although the theory of type A and type B personality is not well considered today, there is still evidence to suggest that different type A traits result in a higher incidence of heart disease, so there is

In conclusion, personality types are observation-based personality models. As long as your model is supported by reality and observation, use it by all means to help others.

Types of thinkers:

The second part of this chapter will examine the different types of thinking styles, first popularized by JP Guilford in his 1955 Structure of The Theory of the Intellect which proposed the original convergent and divergent thinking styles and subsequently modified by others in the field of psychometrics.

Creative thinkers:

Creative thinkers often become artists, musicians, educators, scientists and engineers. They usually respond to negative stimuli by being motivated to solve the problem and produce a positive result.

Logical thinkers:

You can be a logical thinker because you don't think creatively but consider the opposite direction. Individuals who think in this way are often referred to as "hyper thinkers". They tend to break their ideas down into small pieces and dissect each component. It's harder for them to look at their arguments objectively and they don't believe they've missed something.

By compartmentalizing knowledge, they shape a strategy and set small and frequent goals. This type of thinking process considers factual evidence and real objects as elements with respect to theoretical thinking. These thinkers tend to focus on the physical reality and facts in front of them and do not work on supernatural beliefs or forces. While they are good qualities, these can be a weakness, as someone who only thinks concretely may have a hard time understanding new concepts. The mantra of highly logical thinkers is: "What I do not perceive does not happen".

Abstract thinkers:

Abstract thinking is the opposite of concrete thinking. Abstract thinking allows you to theorize and hypothesize. Their reasoning is more of a forecast for the day, believing that something will be as expected, particularly even if it has not yet been observed. A practical thought, on the other hand, can only imagine the day you saw it move and you cannot predict it moving in a direction you have never seen.

Divergent thinkers:

The divergent thinker seeks an innovative path, then expresses his ideas and then contrasts them. They don't necessarily try to match rhythm and performance, rather they look for a special way that is tailored to their particular intent and desire. Sometimes, systemic thinkers or non-linear thinkers imagine the perfect picture. Rather imagine life as a complex and romantic journey than as a direct path to the ultimate goal. To begin with, a rational thinking being would not push themselves to continue on a path that they no longer think is for them. They are open to change and prefer to "punch".

Converging thinkers:

Those who are well coordinated are converging thinkers. Convergent thinking is a method by which several small fragments of knowledge can be collected and combined into a cohesive vision. Such individuals also serve in community departments such as police officers, first aid workers, doctors, nurses, firefighters, and people in military positions. They can process information quickly and efficiently and implement it in a solution.

Convergent thinkers are problem solvers and are often good at English and math. There would always be divergent thinkers, unlike converging thinkers. These people are a bit like converging thinkers as they too often process many thoughts at once. The main difference between the two is that your converging thoughts are the most structured and responsive way they should learn to deal with problems.

Sequential thinkers:
Sequential thinkers or linear thinkers love specific ideas and prefer to re-establish their prescribed paths. For example, you might agree to go to a university your parents attended early, even if you realize it's not for you. Not satisfied with the climate, some people will struggle to change their course in the study, as they have already chosen to take their degree from where you are.

Sequential thinkers prefer to see progress before continuing whatever they are working for so they should feel a very good reason to get them to take that leap to apply for a different college. They often don't reflect on their feelings; they want to see strong evidence that changes their actions.

Generational thinking:
Considering what kind of thinker someone might be. Consider the generation they come from. People of previous generations are closer to each other than younger generations. Fifty years ago, for example, the general American population thought it was unlikely that two people of different ethnicities would meet. Today, this kind of closeness would be regarded by the genetic population as embarrassing and unreasonable. Different generations moralize various things. Older people may be more likely to think your tattoos are obnoxious, as they came from a time when it was common to believe that people with tattoos got

them from a bad life, like going to jail or being a member of a gang. . They were told that a woman who had tattoos was not elegant and that what was probably considered dishonorable work worked. Today, millennials see tattoos primarily as a form of expression and art. You are more likely to consider the cultural importance of tattoos, and it is as a form of therapy for some. You can recognize what people think is important. Learn what not to say around certain types of people, for example, avoid talking about politics around people you know have radical ideas and feelings about government. and it is like a form of therapy for some. You can recognize what people think is important. Learn what not to say around certain types of people, for example, avoid talking about politics around people you know have radical ideas and feelings about government. and it is like a form of therapy for some. You can recognize what people think is important. Learn what not to say around certain types of people, for example, avoid talking about politics around people you know have radical ideas and feelings about government.

Other generic personality types:

To conclude this chapter, we will look at some specific personalities to assist you with the more practical elements of this book.

The dominant person:

A dominant person takes control of a scene. They lead the pack and usually prepare to take the lead. They may not actually fit the group's goal, but they often lead the way. Think back to Chapter 2 and the tamed fox experiment.

Visual contact:

The dominant person communicates dominance through eye contact, but that's not the only way. They are usually free to scroll through the crowd, look at everyone's faces, and aren't afraid to make direct eye contact. They may also be the last person to break eye contact.

Facial expressions:

A dominant person won't smile a lot. He or she may smile from time to time, but it won't always be that warm personal smile. A strong person contrasts his mouth and often frowns, or frowns most of the time if he is one of those he is superior to.

Energy and posture:

We talked before about the posture of power. The dominant individual does this often, making grand gestures and talking to other people as a sign of superiority. It is a show, with the aim of indicating to others the status of the powerful person. People generally take a wider stance and try to look bigger than normal. This is done in a relaxed way: the effort is not strained and everything is a demonstration of domination. When you take a firm handshake, notice that when you shake the dominant person's hand, you are looking directly at their face. Someone who isn't as reliable or anxious will continue to experience quick eye contact. A dominant individual maintains face-to-face orientation and retains the strength of their grip.

Personal space management:

A person of power will consider himself a higher status than others. Of course they also know that such powerful individuals exist. If he or she feels that someone has a lower status, he or she separates from them.

With most people making friends and others with a similar personality, they keep a personal space closer. We are in power position, arms to the side, hands on hips, back straight. Your shoulders may also be a bit set back. Dominant individuals will lead the group and move forward in the group.

Personal interactions:

If a person with power communicates with someone with a weaker personality, they will tend to use touch more often. However, if the dominant person fights others on an equal basis, they both hope to reciprocate. How do you know if this person is impatient? In general, their hands would betray them - and their speech, too, of course. If they speak too fast, and this is combined with a very quick hand gesture, this individual shows a lack of patience. If the movements are still quite choppy, you can be sure.

The overwhelmed worker:

Those who are generally overwhelmed with homework are shaken and demoralized. They will begin to slow down and show signs of resignation and defeat. They got used to their current condition and, at least unconsciously, gave up. These burnt workers have also lost some of their trust and empathy. So how do you help such a person?

Say you are correcting your posture.

Give them an open space. Keep your torso open: arms and hands on your hips and face when you speak. This shows empathy not only with their bodily expressions, but also with their facial expressions. You will be careful: look at the expanded pupils. Listen to them with intent and empathize where appropriate. You will also notice that from time to time, they are usually hand to heart.

Shy individuals:

Sometimes the shy types of wallflower are easy to spot. They don't talk much for one thing, but how do you know if someone just doesn't want to be at the bar or if that person is really a wallpaper? Here are some tips that can help. When a shy guy seems to be holding his glass protectively in the bar. It would be as if someone were afraid to take him away. A strong sign is that they normally cover their hands. Why is it? Glass (or whatever is used as a facade) is just a social crutch. They never run out of their drinks, they keep their inspections: their bikes, eyes and hands are always on their phones and it's like they're the only companion they have. They model and drink like everyone else does, but they never start anything. When these individuals approach, they do it in a gentle way. Even compliments that seem understated are sensitive to everything. Help them warm up in the crowd, and in a way, you can help them develop their confidence.

Chapter 8 : your mind and the way you communicate

Much of an individual's communication is not based solely on what they are actively trying to publish. A much larger and much more active part of our communication is based on what we do not realize we are spreading around the world. Our body can reveal our deepest emotions and feelings without us realizing it practically twenty-four sects. This doesn't happen randomly, of course. The way our mind communicates without us realizing it is based on two main theories of thought. These are known as the unconscious mind and the limbic brain. In the next chapter I will define and give the importance of the unconscious mind and the limbic brain in our communication.

Unconscious mind

The unconscious mind originates from Freud's psychoanalytic theory of personality. In this theory, Freud defines the unconscious mind as a hidden well of feelings, thoughts, impulses and memories that are separate from our conscious awareness of feelings. The contents of our unconscious mind tend to be unpleasant or depressing. They tend to include feelings of pain, anxiety, or conflict. It is because of these negative feelings and emotions that our unconscious mind remains outside of our conscious awareness. Since on a subconscious level, we don't want to remember or experience those feelings, so let's try to ignore them and push them into our unconscious mind.

Despite this attempt to ignore and hide these feelings, our unconscious mind still influences our behavior even if we don't know it's there. Many people compare the unconscious mind to that of an iceberg. The part of the iceberg that sits above the water represents our conscious brain and all the communication of ideas and feelings that we actively spread around the world. On the contrary, our unconscious mind is represented by every part of the iceberg that is under water and invisible. Within this iceberg analogy, it is important to remember how big an iceberg really is under water. This represents how deep our unconscious mind is and how much it tends to be hidden beneath the surface.

Freud also believed and stated that our basic instincts and animal drives are contained in the unconscious mind. This includes the instincts under actions of life and death as well as the sexual instincts. He believed that impulses like these were hidden or expelled from our current consciousness because our minds consider them unacceptable, irrational or uncivilized. Freud has suggested that individuals often use a variety of different defense mechanisms to prevent these hidden impulses from rising above the waters in our conscious mind.

Freud also goes on to explain the different ways in which information from the unconscious mind could be brought into conscious awareness. One of the techniques Freud explained can be used to bring these feelings to awareness is known as free association. Free association is a rather simple and seemingly silly form of psychotherapy. In free association, Freud asked patients to stretch out and relax and tell him whatever came to mind without any kind of filter. He wanted them to say anything they could think of without stopping to think it was trivial, irrelevant or embarrassing. Freud then traced the flows of thoughts until he believed he could discover the contents of the unconscious mind.

Freud also believes that dream interpretation could be used to further understand the unconscious mind. Many people think of dreams as a path to the unconscious mind and believe that information from the unconscious mind may appear randomly in dreams, but typically in a disguised format. For this reason, he often asked patients to keep dream journals and tried to read and interpret these dreams to try to understand their hidden meanings.

Freud also believes that dreams tended to serve as a form of secret satisfaction of long-cherished wishes. He believes that the fact that these unconscious impulses were not expressed in real life means that they could be expressed in the individual's dreams.

Freud's theory of the unconscious mind has not been without controversy. A multitude of researchers have criticized the idea of the unconscious mind and strongly deny that there is no unconscious mind at all. Recently, in the field of cognitive psychology, researchers and psychologists have begun to focus on automatic and instinctive functions that describe things that were previously attributed to the unconscious mind. The ideas behind this approach believe that there are a number of cognitive functions that occur outside of our conscious awareness.

Meanwhile, they do not fully support the vocal conceptualization of the unconscious mind, but they do offer some evidence that actions we are not aware of still have an influence on our automatic behaviors. Unlike Freud's psychoanalytic approaches to the unconscious mind, research in the modern field of cognitive psychology is driven almost exclusively by scientific inquiry and quantitative data. This idea of the unconscious mind continues to have a great effect on modern psychology and is still used in some modern practices today.

The limbic system within an individual's brain is responsible for a variety of very important brain functions. The greatest responsibility of the limbic system is our instinct for survival and for accessing and storing memory. The limbic system is made up of many different brain structures: two of the largest and most important parts of the limbic system are the amygdala and the hippocampus. The amygdala is the deciding structure that chooses where each memory is to be placed in the brain, while the hippocampus transports that memory to its final location. Placement is often believed to be determined by the amount of emotional response the person receives.

The limbic system is also very responsible for hormone levels, body temperature and motor functions. The different parts of the limbic brain system are the amygdala, the cingulate gyrus, the hippocampus and the hypothalamus. These individual structures are very important parts of a person's brain. The limbic system as a whole is found in the upper part of the brain stem and below the frontal cortex. The limbic system is often linked to survival-based emotions such as fear, anger, and pleasure. The limbic system is also known to affect both the peripheral nervous system and the endocrine system. The part of the limbic system that is important for this text, in particular, is its connection with memory. Due to the The perceived importance of the limbic system in making decisions about where memories go and how they are remembered is often connected to Freud's ideas of the unconscious mind. Since Freud's ideas of the unconscious mind are based on the theory that certain memories and feelings are hidden away from our conscious awareness, it is easy to understand how the limbic system can play a huge role in this, considering that it is believed to be the deciding factor. where our memories are stored. Now, you might be thinking to yourself, "What does all of this have to do with our body language and understanding the body language of those around us?" The answer lies in the fact that the unconscious mind is very powerful and controls a huge part of our true feelings and emotions. By reading body language, we can often unlock these feelings of the unconscious mind without even realizing that they are hidden from the person we are reading. This is a very powerful skill and it is important to understand the basics. The limbic system and the unconscious mind create this basis for people's deeper readings.

Chapter 9: complexity of the face

Returning to our non-verbal communication methods and body language reading, we come to the complexities and extreme complications of facial communication. The face is a huge indicator of non-verbal communication within body language. The face tends to tell everything. The face is also the hardest to control when trying to regulate one's body language. In this chapter, we will discuss the use of the face as a method for non-verbal communication and how we can easily read it for ourselves. We will also analyze the expressive parts of the face and what they can say in terms of non-verbal communication.

Many parts of the face are the first things we consider when looking at a new person. For this reason, a lot can be transmitted on a person's face. This is partly an evolutionary result because we spend so much time looking at the faces of those around us to the point that, over time, we have evolved to be able to convey emotions and expressions on their faces in a way that those around us they didn't ask to know what we're feeling. There are a few tricks for reading someone's face besides a simple basis for determining whether or not they are angry with you.

The first is to stare into an individual's eyes. When you start reading a person's face, you will want to start with their eyes. The eyes contain the greatest expression in a person's face. You can learn an extreme amount of detail about someone's emotions by paying close attention to their eyes. Later in the chapter, we will look at some common expressions that we can read in the eye.

The next step is to look at the lips. The muscles of our lips are extremely sensitive and change constantly. A person's lips can move and react to situations without an individual even realizing what they are doing. You can pay attention to a person's lip to understand how they feel about certain situations or what their next action might be.

The next step may come as a surprise to most people. This is to pay attention to the nose. The nose doesn't change as much as the eyes and lips, but its position on the face makes it a very important part of face reading. The nose is right in the center of a person's face. It is for this reason that many people tend to look at a person's nose before they even look at a person's eyes or mouth. For this reason, the nose acts as a base or central location for the rest of our face. If an event or sensation is powerful enough to make the nose move, then you can take it as a sign that whatever happened was revolutionary enough to shift the very foundation of that person's face.

The next step and the part of the face to pay attention to is the eyebrows. Linked to the eyes and often to the more expressive second parts of our face, the eyebrows can express a wide variety of emotions. Their ability to move with a great level of dexterity and reach puts them at a greater advantage over the rest of our face. Furthermore, our brows tend to work in connection with our eyes. So, by taking the eyes and eyebrows as a whole, you can get a complete picture of a person's emotions or feelings about a certain event.

The final step in being able to correctly and accurately read a person's face is to simply acquire the ability to perceive different emotions on the face. We will discuss this in more detail later in this chapter as I expose the different emotions that various expressions tend to exhibit.

The head is often the first thing a person looks at when meeting a new individual. We spend most of our life looking at a person's head. As a result, the human head is designed to send many signals between individuals. Most of them tend to be subconscious, which is useful in the context of this book.

- *The face*

    The human face contains about fifty muscles; most of these muscles can be used to send non-verbal signals to those around us. In addition to muscles, skin color and temperature can also be very important in understanding non-verbal language from the face.

    - Color: Face colors tell a long, detailed story about what a person is feeling at a given point. If a person's face is very clearly red, they may be showing signs for many different things. In very general terms, a red face is a sign that someone's face is hot. Whether it's exercise, emotional arousal, or embarrassment, it's a sign that blood is running down your face for one reason or another. It can also be a sign of anger or aggression. Alternatively, the face color can also be white. A whiteness of the skin can be a sign of cold and blood coming out of the face. This can be a sign of illness or fear. A face can also take on a bluish tinge when it is very cold or in extreme fear or disease.

    - Humidity: The level of humidity that someone's face has when you look at it can tell a wide variety of feelings. You need to be careful not to look too far into this sign, as wetness on a person's face can also be caused by simply sweating when it's hot outside. If the area a person is in is not hot and their face appears to be very humid or covered with a lot of moisture, that person may be afraid, as sweat is often associated with fear. Some scientists theorize that sweating on the face when fear is felt is an evolutionary defense mechanism to make the skin slippery and more difficult for an opponent to gain a firm grip on the face.

The following are a number of common facial cues that indicate different emotions. It is important to remember that some of these signs are not an instant indicator that a person is experiencing the emotion in question. However, a combination of all of these signs can suggest that a person is experiencing a certain emotion, depending on the environment around them.

- *Common signs of happiness*

  Some common signs of happiness within the face include but are not limited to:

  - The mouth and an open or closed smile sometimes accompanied by laughter or giggles;
  - Perhaps some crow's feet-like wrinkles on the sides of a person's eyes: this indicates that a smile is honest and real because it uses enough muscle to change a person's wrinkles and face; Slightly raised eyebrows; is

- *Common signs of sadness*

  Some common signs of sadness within the face and head include but are not limited to:

  - A person's eyes look down at an angle of less than ninety degrees;
  - Maybe some dampness or moisture inside the eyes;
  - Head tilted down together with the eyes;
  - Lips clench tightly or tremble;
  - Tremor of the chin and the head tilted to
  - the side.

- *Common signs of anxiety*

Some common signs of anxiety within the face and head include but are not limited to:

- Wet or damp eyes
- Eyebrows joined and curled;
- A lower lip trembles or lips pinch;
- Skin wrinkles or tightness is

Head tilted down, possibly looking at the ground.

- *Common signs of fear*

Some common signs of fear within the face and head include but are not limited to:

- Wide eyes with large pupils;
- Eyes closed or pointed down
- Eyebrows raised by curling the forehead;
- The open mouth or the corners of the mouth rotate
- downward;
- Chin pulled and hidden in the neck;

Head tilted downwards possibly fixing the ground; and A face painted in white.

- *Common signs of anger*

Some common signs of anger include but are not limited to:

- Eyes wide open and fixed or half closed
- Eyebrows push down towards the eyes and perhaps forever
- A wrinkled forehead
- Nostrils that widen or contract

A mouth that is flattened in a line or clearly clenched teeth

An edge protruding towards a person

- A red face

- *Common signs of envy or jealousy*

Some common signs of envy or jealousy within the face and head include but are not limited to:

- Wide eyes with large pupils
- The corners of the mouth turn downwards
- Puckering of the nose or mockery of an individual
- Chin protruding outward from the body

- *Common signs of desire or lust*

Common signs of desire or lust within the face and head include but are not limited to:

- Wide eyes with strongly dilated pupils;
- Slightly raised but soft eyebrows;
- Lips slightly parted or curled;
- Stop smiling; is

Head that is tilted forward or slightly tilted to the side.

- *Common signs of interest*

Some common signs of interest include but are not limited to:

- A fixed gaze at the object or person in question. Squinting in the eye may also occur as a person tries to better see the object or person in question
- Slightly raised eyebrows
- Lips pressed tightly together
- Head straight or push forward slightly with your neck

stretching your lips in a soft or gentle smile

- *Common signs of boredom*

Some common signs of boredom within the face and head may include but are not limited to:

- Eyes that look away from the object or individual in
- question;
- Face generally motionless but relaxed;

The corners of the mouth are turned down or the lips pulled to the side; is

- Head supported with one hand or supported in some other way.

- *Common signs of relief*

Some common signs of relief within the face and head include but are not limited to:

- The eyebrows are tilted outward or lowered on the outer edges and higher on the inner edges;

- A mouth that is slightly open or smiling is. A head tilted up in surprise.

- *Common signs of surprise*

Some common signs of surprise within the face and head include but are not limited to:

- Eyes wide dilated pupils;
- The eyebrows push up on the head with extreme wrinkles of the forehead;

- Open mouth with a lower chin; is. Head that is tilted back or tilted to the side.

- *Common signs of disgust*

  Some common signs of disgust within the face and head include but are not limited to:

  - Head or eyes away from the object or person in question
  - Opening of the nostrils or contraction of the nose
  - Puckered nose or snoring mouth
  - Closed mouth
  - Maybe the tongue sticks out

  Chin protruding from the neck and body

- *Common signs of shame*

  Some common signs of shame on the face and head include but are not limited to:

  - The head or eyes turn downward when
  - looking at the ground; Eyebrows low on the face but
  - not strongly; e The skin may be bright red or red.

- *Common signs of pity*

  Some common signs that someone feels pity for another individual within the face and head include but are not limited to:

  - Look away, possibly with some dampness or humidity;
  - Eyebrows joined slightly in the center or pulled down at the edges;

  Wooden corners of the mouth pointing downwards; is

  - Add maybe tilted to the side or tilted forward slightly.

- *Common signs of calm*

Some common signs that someone is feeling very calm about an event or situation within the face and head include but are not limited to:

- Relaxed facial muscles;
- Fixed gaze that looks ahead with the eyes; is
- The mouth may be raised slightly to the sides in a slight smile.

In this section, we will discuss how to somehow come to those around us. If you want to make someone believe that you are a certain type of individual, these are some of the things you want to think about.

Reliability

Psychologists and body language experts have agreed that many people believe that the most trustworthy face is one that appears to have a slight smile. These individuals will have the corners of their mouth turned slightly upward with the eyebrows just raised to the face. You must remember that the eyebrows do not have to be strongly raised with many wrinkles on the forehead. These characteristics show that an individual appears confident and friendly but without being overbearing or scared of others not like them.

Intelligence

Many scientists and body language experts have agreed that people with narrower faces and thinner chins tend to be smarter than others. In addition to this, people also tend to see those with larger noses as a common stereotype of how smart a person can be. Conversely, an individual with an oval face and a large chin is often stereotyped as having lower intelligence levels. Interestingly, it has also been shown that people tend to perceive others as having a higher intelligence when one individual smiles or shows happiness, while people tend to judge others as having lower intelligence when they show signs of anger or happiness. sadness. You can artificially seem smarter by using some body language power signs. Signs of body language power include things like speaking expressively,

The chin is a dominant and obvious angle of the face. All corners of the face have their own clear body language symbols which are unique to them. This is because a corner of your face is an area where its different parts converge and, as such, it is the beginning and the end of some facial expressions. In this section, we will explain the intentional or unintentional meanings behind certain chin movements.

- Protection: The chin is a very vulnerable point on the face, as it tends to protrude and it becomes easy to attack with fists. The chin sits just above the throat, which is an even more vulnerable spot. The chin can often act as a throat protector in cases of extreme vulnerability. There, they may feel defensive for some reason. Holding the chin also tends to lower the head, which then tends to be a submissive gesture. This is different from the defensive move we discussed earlier because the head is tilted down and because the eyes are often fixed on the ground. This can be considered a shy or flirtatious movement.

- Putting out: The chin can be a subtle method of pointing to other things. Hitting the chin or tilting the head can give a slight signal that only conscious people will notice. Putting your chin out towards a person means exposing it and sending a message that is challenging a person to attack it. This is often considered a sign of challenge. It is often believed that men with larger chins have more testosterone than others. For this reason, the action of a man with a very large chin cropping it enhances this idea by giving a mental symbol to those around them who are*alpha*. It is often the case that if a person feels more confident than normal, their chin will protrude slightly because they hold their head high or perhaps tilt their head back a little. Pushing the chin outward also tends to expose the teeth and this can be considered a threat because they may subconsciously want to bite another person.

- Touching: When an individual is seen stroking their chin, it is often regarded as a signal that the person is thinking very long and hard. They can judge or evaluate a person or situation. If a conversation offeredthem a choice or a decision to make, they can take this action to show that they are thinking about it. The head is one of the heaviest parts of our body and is supported solely by the neck and spine. This can cause a lot of exhaustion and tension, and as a result, people are often seen cupping their heads in their hands. This can be a sign of boredom or sleepiness. A more complicated symbol shown by holding the chin is to prevent the head from moving. This can show that the individual in question unconsciously wants to send a particular signal to the head but does not want to send the signal at the same time due to some kind of logical reasoning.

- Beard: Beards have a very interesting connotation in terms of body language. In our society, the shaved beard tends to be the most widely accepted form of facial hair. Hence, in modern society, the beard is sometimes considered a sign that an individual is a non-conformist. A person with a full, sensual beard is more likely to be regarded as a person with no need for vanity and is usually considered confident and relaxed. On the other hand, when a beard is styled and kept very neatly, it can show that a person is vain and more fussy than a normal individual. If the beard is viewed as matted or growing very wildly around an individual space, people might take it as a sign that the said guy is messy or tends to be sloppy. L'

- Curled: A chin that is seen as curled or pulled in particular directions and that looks wrinkled can be seen as a defensive position because it can be put under the general idea of pulling the chin back.

The mouth

The mouth is a very important aspect of our face. It probably has the most muscles of any other region of our face and, as such, is used to convey the most complex forms of body language as well as verbal language.

when we need more oxygen than usual, we can use our mouth to breathe in larger bursts of air. If an individual suddenly begins to breathe through their mouth at a fast enough rate almost to the point of panting, they may be seen as scared or angry because they are subconsciously preparing for the fight or flight reaction. The breathing of a stressed person can include actions such as swallowing a large burst of air or expelling it very quickly. If a person is extremely and overwhelmingly stressed, they may begin to hyperventilate. When an individual yawns, it is often considered a sign that a person is tired or bored. If an individual gives a short or deep sigh, it can be seen as a sign of sadness or frustration. L'

- Speaking: A mouth tends to send even more signals while speaking than traditional verbal language. If a mouth moves very little and includes murmuring, this could be a sign that an individual doesn't want to talk, which could be stemming from shyness or a fear of revealing too much about something. Moving very fast and a lot, at the same time someone is speaking, can indicate that they are experiencing extreme levels of arousal or domination. People who speak very fast tend to be visual thinkers who try to say what they see as quickly as possible. An individual who speaks very slowly can be considered a deep thinker and perhaps tries to be careful in finding the correct words.

- Eating: The way people eat can tell a lot about their personality. A person who looks very high manners and greetings will open their mouth as little as possible to put in a small amount of food and keep it closed while chewing carefully. These individuals will never speak when they have food in their mouth. Conversely, a person who does not take good hands into high regard will push large mouthfuls into his wide mouth and will tend to chew and talk at the same time. Interestingly, there are some people who turn these trends into their heads by eating very loudly as a sign that they are enjoying their food. These people are very snobbish about their food choices.

- Cover: Sometimes, people use their hands to cover their mouths. In modern society, exposing the insides of the mouth can be considered rude in some environments, so the hand is used to cover the mouth when yawning or laughing out loud.

- Smile: the smile has a very interesting depth to which it transmits emotions. Many people will look at a smile and just think that it is conveying the fact that someone is happy, when in reality a smile can mean many different things, depending on the context. A full smile is one that uses the entire face - this type of smile will include the eyes, cheeks and eyebrows. The eyes will fold, the eyebrows will rise and the cheeks will lift the words. If an individual smiles only with his lips, he often tries to deceive another individual. These smiles are typically fakes that are not to be trusted. A genuine smile, on the other hand, tends to be asymmetrical and is usually much larger on one side of the face. If an individual has a lopsided smile, it is very likely that he is a reliable person. However, if an individual smiles with tight lips, they may show signs of embarrassment. If an individual only smiles halfway down their mouth on one side of their face, they may be showing sarcasm or uncertainty.

- Laugh: There are many different types of laughter in this world. Each has its own meanings and signals in the realm of body language. Laughing can sometimes act as a kind of bonding mechanism between men and women. It is well known that women tend to laugh at the men they love, while men have fun when women laugh at them. It is said to be a woman who laughs at a man a sign that she likes. Laughing can also be used to send signals that one sees the other in terms of friendship. Laughing at jokes is often a requirement if you are friends with the person making the joke. Laughing or smiling at the misfortune of those around us is often considered unacceptable in our society. Since we are human beings, we often can't help but find some unfortunate events amusing. Because of this, you may see repressed laughter or people trying very hard not to smile as someone experiences one of these unfortunate events.

- Biting or Sucking: An individual sucking our finger is often a reminder of our childhood actions, as we tend to suck our thumbs when we were children. Young children will suck their fingers as a breast substitute. For this reason, this action is considered comforting. This can be a sign that a person is feeling uncomfortable or stressed in a particular situation and that they are simply trying to console themselves by sucking their fingers, which brings them back to that comforting feeling of having a breast in their mouth when they were. a child. The variance on this includes actions such as sucking or biting the knuckles, the side of the hands, or other parts of the body. Sometimes, this can include the lips or the inside of the cheek. Sometimes, this includes an external object like a pen or pencil.

The nose

Within this section, we will look at the common signals sent by the nose. Since the nose is positioned right in the center of the face, it can send out a large number of body symbols.

- Flare: When the nostrils have been widened and flared, it allows an individual to breathe in more oxygen. Unconsciously, this is an act of preparing a person for combat. For this reason, this may indicate that an individual is experiencing extreme sorrow or perhaps feels threatened.

- Wrinkles: If a nose is wrinkled, it could be a sign that a person is feeling a bad smell from a certain area. It can also be a metaphor for the arrival of something bad. An example of this is when an individual suggests something that another person doesn't like, they might wrinkle their nose at that idea. Another variation of this idea is whether a person is thinkingsomething or have certain ideas but I am not satisfied with those ideas or thoughts.

- Touch: When an individual touches their nose, it can be a sign that a person detects a terrible smell. It can also seem like a common signal from a person who is lying. Touching the nose indicates someone is lying when combined with the right combination of other body symbols. If a person makes a quick gesture, know that this could be a sign that they disagree with something a previous person said. If an individual pinches the bridge of their nose, they may be thinking very hard about something. Usually, this is combined with some kind of frustration, as a person may have a hard time making a decision. Putting a finger on the nose or pressing it is sometimes a natural habit or tick a person has when they think very deeply about something.

- Look Up: When an individual is seen looking up, they often think very hard about a certain idea. When they are giving a prepared speech or presentation, they may try to remember the prepared words if they look up. Looking up and to the left can show signs that someone is trying to recall a memory.

  Conversely, someone looking up and to the right may show signs of imaginative construction, which then shows that they are inventing something on the spot. Searching can also be considered a sign of boredom, as a person is trying to examine or understand their surroundings to find something better to do. If a person's head is lowered and if their eyes are looking at another person through their lashes, this can be considered a koi and a suggestion for action, as it is used in conjunction with the idea of submission with the head down. and eye contact of attraction. However, when combined with a frown, this can be considered a critical look.

  trust, power or domination. If a person looks at another person, they may show a sign of submission. This can also be a sign that a person is feeling particularly guilty. If a person looks down and to the left, it could be a sign that they are trying to talk to themselves without being noticed. However, if an individual looks down and to the right, this could be a sign that he is dealing with certain internal emotions or internal turmoil at the moment. There are some cultures and societies where direct eye contact is considered a rude or dominant symbol. For this reason, people in these societies can look down while talking to others to show respect.

- Looking sideways: Most of our vision tends to be in the horizontal plane. So if an individual appears to be looking sideways, it means that they are actively turning their head to see something they would not have already seen. A quick sideways glance is sometimes considered a symbol that someone is just looking for the source of a distraction. This can also be considered a sign of irritation. If a person looks directly to the left, this may indicate that a person is trying to recall a sound in their memory. On the other hand, looking to the right can show that a person imagines a

sound. If a person's eyes are moving rapidly from side to side, this can be a sign that a person should not be trusted or that they are lying.
This goes back to the idea that an individual is looking for an escape route in the event that he is discovered or attacked.

- Looking: The act of looking is a sign that someone is very interested in understanding whatever they are looking at by staring at something with the intent of trying to understand it on a deeper level. This can be a sign that one individual is very interested in another. If, after making eye contact with another person, a person continues to look into their eyes, it could be a sign of love. If the eyes slide over the individual's body, it is more likely to be a sign of lust. Where the eyes go is important. Looking at a person's mouth can indicate that a person would like to kiss them. Looking at individual sexual regions tends to show a desire to have intercourse with that person. Slide your eyes up and down an ' whole person is usually considered an act of sizing an individual. This can be viewed as a potential threat or as seeking a sexual partner, depending on where the eyes linger. This can be considered an insult in modern society.

As we can see from the contents of this chapter, the face and head of an individual's body contain some of the most expressive and powerful forms of body language. In this chapter, we have examined the meanings of various different forms of body language that exclusively include the connection between head and face. It is important to remember that when trying to analyze the actions of a person's head or face, all parts and angles of that person's face must be taken into consideration. You cannot judge a person's emotions simply through an action of a part of their face. You have to take their face into consideration as a whole and consider all the possible meanings for all the different parts. For this chapter, we examined and analyzed the different expressions and meanings behind certain movements of eyes, smiles, lips, and many others. In the next chapter, we will begin by explaining how you can tell if there is truth in your relationships.

The forehead is often ignored in the realm of body language. This is a huge mistake, as the forehead is often a starting point for a wider range of body language signals. It is just above the eyes and, as such, can be looked at without sending out different signals. Many people, when they want to prevent people from reading the signs on their foreheads, wear a large hat and keep their heads down. This is particularly common in gamblers.

- Wrinkles: If a forehead is wrinkled, it is often due to an individual's eyebrow movement. For this reason, forehead wrinkles act as an amplifier of the eyebrow signals. This can indicate surprise or questioning.

- Sweating: As humans, we often excrete sweat on the head earlier than on other parts of our body. Sweating on the forehead not only occurs when we are hot due to the outside temperature but also when we havethey are hot due to internal energy and excitement. It is important to remember that an individual can also experience what is known as cold sweat, which then indicates large amounts of fear and can be accompanied by moisture in the eye.

- Touching: Forehead rubbing is often considered a form of body language that means a greeting. Slowly rubbing your forehead may tend to indicate deep thought or deep contemplation. If an individual is seen rubbing their temples on both sides, this can be a sign of stress or an oncoming headache.

Chapter 10 How to identify insecurity

Insecurity means that a person does not feel safe. Insecure people constantly have the nagging feeling that they are not safe, accepted and agree with who they are. The biggest problem with insecurity is that it doesn't come out as clearly as we talk about it because no one wants to admit that he or she lives in constant worry and fear. Therefore, people work very hard to mask or cover their anxiety with habitual behaviors that very often work against them. The things they do get them the opposite results from what they were looking for.

In case you are unsure if someone is insecure or you feel insecure, below are some of the signs of insecurity you may recognize: Signs of insecurity

He or she talks about the appearance of other people

Someone who doesn't like how it sounds will often point to someone else in the room, on social media, or even at the gym. He or she will talk about how the other person looks awful, ugly, has awful clothes, and what they should have done to look better. This is because the person wants to take away the attention that he assumes that others are giving it from himself to the other person he has identified.

He cares and guesses himself in everything

An insecure person will be worried about everything he does. Everything. If he gives a speech, he will be worried that his voice was not loud enough, his laugh was too long, or that people were not taking notes while he was speaking for which he will wonder if they got anything from what he said. If the person mops the floor, they will be worried that they did it in a way that didn't impress other people. When wearing clothes, he will wonder if he is dressed too light or too heavy for the occasion. While it's common to ask one or two people what they think about your outfit, the insecure person will want to know what everyone in the room is feeling. The higher the number, the better it is for his confidence.

Keep pushing back and pulling back

An insecure person will want to drag you in, and as you get closer, the person will suddenly freak out and push you further. The individual will do so fearing rejection. He'll want to take you away soon enough so that you don't get a chance to do it to him. Amazingly, once you are away, the person will start begging you to come back.

The person continually tries to know if you are crazy and if what he did made you angry.

Insecurity will have a person constantly asking you if something they did made you angry. He or she lives in constant worry of losing you and they think that if they don't do what you want, how you want them to be done, you will leave their life.

It seems the whole world hates them

One of the most obvious signs of an insecure person, which emerges in many of the insecure people, is to think that every other person hates them. If you ask them why, the person can't point out anything in particular that people don't like and they can't tell you how they know. All the person is sure of is that people on this earth hate him.

He is concerned that someone might speak ill of him or her

Insecure people are always worried that people are talking about them behind their backs. They are constantly afraid of being despised and this insecurity leads them to seek confirmation that the people around them are not speaking badly to them. Usually, there's no reason to even talk about it. Brags to others An insecure person wants others to know about the accomplishments they have achieved in life or career. He wants everyone to know the beautiful lady he is dating or who has just bought the latest model of car. Don't confuse bragging with trust or as social media calls it "counting my blessings." This is simply pride. People who are happy with who they are, what they have done, what is happening in their life and the miles they have traveled have no reason to brag.

He humiliates the people he once knew

A person who is unsure of how they have treated or behaved towards another person will try to speak badly or publicly defame the other person. Even worse, the person will only offer the side of the story that portrays him as a good person. People who have not made a mistake or played a role that contributed to the downfall of the relationship or friendship have no interest in ruining another person's reputation. Indeed, people with emotional intelligence and integrity don't care about the scandals that are raised, they just ignore them or try to solve their problems in private.

He has an excuse to step on others

A person who is fully aware of wasting other people's time and resources by treating people like disposable items will always find a good reason to do so. For example, if the person shows up an hour late, doesn't treat their family and friends with love, or talks behind another person's back, they'll find a way to justify their behavior. Upon hearing their apology, you will notice that they look noble, but they are not. If you turn around and question this person, they will turn you into an idiot.

It belittles the success of others

An insecure person, driven by the spirit of competition, listens to the praise of another person's success, feels that people consider the other person's success to be superior to what they have achieved, and is intimidated by success begins to try to belittle and belittle the other person's superior results in the best possible way.

However, a person who celebrates the success of others and uses them as inspiration to push himself to achieve greater things is comfortable with who he is and cannot be considered insecure. He doesn't need to reinforce it with the guys to prove he's powerful too.

It wins horribly

An insecure person preemptively hits your wins and works hard to cover the losses they have made in the past. In this way, the person will try to dispel any kind of doubts that others around him have regarding his abilities. A good winner has nothing to prove to others. They only enjoy their participation in the activity and, when all is over, they disappear into their private life without disturbing others with presumptuous speeches.

Loses badly

Just as insecure people are poor winners, they are also poor losers. There is nothing an insecure person hates more than losing. People may call it determination, but it's just a ploy to hide their losses. When the person fails, he makes speeches about how manipulative the system is or how the person who won cheated. They will also complain about how the person who won got an unfair advantage and how the insecure person watched the exercise for a long time without speaking.

He makes fun of the poor

A person who is unsure of his level of financial security will sincerely and constantly ridicule those living in poverty and adverse conditions. People who don't define themselves by the amount they earn have no business insulting and mocking those whose wages are low.

Make unnecessary threats

Most of the time, when an insecure person realizes that their insecurities have been discovered, or at least that they are suspicious, they make threats. If you go ahead and test the person's insecurity and primitive ways of acting, the person starts threatening you with your job, your reputation, and the relationships you have. A person who is confident in who he is will have no reason to get angry when people know some things about him or her, even the mistakes he has made, because the person believes those are learning moments.

He does not see positivity in others

A person who is intimidated by another person's accomplishments, greatness and good name begins to work to bring that other person down. He or she will frantically look for whatever negative thing you have done and then point it out to other people. His joy will be ensuring that those who respect you know all the negative information and weaknesses you have. Surprisingly, the person will stay away from strengths and good things you have done or said.

Anything that is said or done is secretly an attack on him

A person who is so insecure and unable to hide it will think that everything you do or say is a direct hit intended to attack them individually. For example, if you have the insecure person for a husband and you stay out late with your girlfriends, once you get back, he will start wondering if you stayed out late trying to prove to others that he has no friends but you do. Actually, staying out late had nothing to do with your partner at least.

An insecure person will also think that everything that is said around them has ulterior motives and will constantly scramble the conversation to himself in an attempt to unravel the motives of everyone involved.

He insists on having the last word

Many insecure people like to engage others in a battle of words as a way to feel intelligent, authoritative, validated, and to feel like they have been heard. As a result, the person will not concede in an argument, even when he sees that the other person's argument makes sense, and his or her no longer does. However, stupid is his argument, the person will make sure he gets the last word, otherwise he will feel insignificant and inferior.

He wants to bring up your past mistakes and put them on you

Some people use their mistakes and failures as a way to define themselves that won't let you get over yours. They look for an opportunity to talk about a mistake you made or a time when your life wasn't what it is now, and they'll let everyone know. Their job is to get everyone labeled you for that mistake so that people consider the person better than you, or at least equal to you. A person with this character is not moved by any good thing that you have done or accomplished; the negative aspects of your life matter the most to him or her.

"Humblebrag"

A humblebrag is ordinary bragging disguised in a self-derogatory statement. There are too many of them on social media platforms. For example, someone will complain about the long flight they had to endure, but they will be grateful that at least the person was first class. Another will complain about how he has to take his children to expensive places because they ask him and he is too weak to say no. Another will complain about how he had to spend the weekend watching his son's hockey games, but that he is so grateful that the best players of the season have emerged. Too many people on the Internet have tried to humbly brag to gloat over their successes.

He occasionally reminds other people of his achievements

You will quickly take note of an insecure person by listening to their speech because the person keeps talking about the things they have accomplished. This is an attempt to remind you that under no circumstances should you take this lightly. The person will talk about the lifestyle he has managed to achieve on his own, how he has raised smart children who now run large organizations around the world, and how long he has supported a marriage so that you know he is good at relationships. You will also be constantly reminded how young he was when he made his first million dollars.

Statements like these are the person's way of remembering their worth and making sure you won't forget it too.

Also try to make yourself insecure

The moment you start questioning your self-esteem, realize that it is because of the company you have started to keep. Evaluate the people around your life and see if any of them continue to convey their results to the point that you feel inferior. If you don't usually feel inferior, but are now starting to do so, chances are that the insecure people you've added to your life have started projecting their insecurities at you.

Complains about how bad things are (or how they have yet to get to a certain level)

People with an inferiority complex will want you to see how high their standards are; you may be tempted to think they are snobbish. However, realize that the person is only acting to charm you and make you realize that he is better than you. It may become difficult to shake this feeling. By the high standards they proclaim, insecure people intend to show others that they are better than you because they adhere to higher self-assessment criteria.

The ability to detect the insecurity that people around you project will help you get rid of the self-doubts that being with people like them has implanted in you. If you can avoid interacting with insecure people in your life, do so. Cut the relationship you have with them. If people are close to you, take the high road and don't give in to these feelings so that you can cultivate the sense of fulfillment only through what you do, not by comparing your results with those of other people.

Chapter 11 How to spot the lie

The fact is that only 54% of lies can be accurately detected. Research has also shown that extroverts tell more lies than introverts, and no less than 82% of lies usually go undetected.

However, the good news is that people can also improve their lie detection skills, maximizing accuracy by up to 90%. The big question here is how to detect that someone is lying. One of the first steps in this whole process is to understand how someone generally acts, especially when they speak.

Basically, this is the processing process known as the baseline. A baseline is essentially the way a person acts when they are in non-threatening and just normal conditions. According to the Science of People website, it's basically the way a person looks when they're telling the truth. To make it clearer, it might be a little hard to tell when a person isn't saying the fact if you're not sure how they usually behave when they're telling the truth, which, to a broader extent, makes a lot of sense.

However, the techniques used to determine if someone is lying can be confusing. In fact, these strategies can also be very conflicting. For this reason, it's important to think twice before making an accusation, make sure you hear yourself more than once to do so, unless it's important to go ahead and find out what happened. Here are some of the telltale signs that someone is not telling the truth;

Behavioral delay or pause

It starts when you ask someone a question and initially get no response. The person then starts responding after a certain delay. There is a big question that should be asked here; how long must the delay extend before it becomes significant before it can be considered a misleading sign? However, it depends on a few factors. You can try this particular exercise on a friend and ask a question like this: "What were you doing on a day like this six years ago.

After asking this question, you will notice that the person will pause constantly before answering the question. This is because it is not a type of question that naturally evokes a quick and immediate response. Even if the person takes time to think about the question, they may still not be able to give a meaningful answer. The next question to ask would be, "Six years ago did you rob a clothing store on this day?" if they pause before giving you the answer you need, it would be very important to choose wisely what kind of friends you have.

In most cases, there will be no pause and the person is likely to respond simply by saying no and letting the story die.

This is a simple test that tends to bring home the point that delays should usually be considered outside of God's church. In the context of oneself; is appropriate for the question under consideration.

Verbal or non-verbal disconnection

The human brain has been wired in such a way that both non-verbal and verbal behaviors match naturally. Hence, whenever there is a disconnection, it is usually considered a very important deceptive indicator. A very common verbal or non-verbal disconnect that you should pay attention to occurs when someone nods in the affirmative while answering "No". It could also occur when a person moves their head from one end to the other when they answer "Yes".

If you were to perform that mismatch, for example, to offer an answer to a question, then you will realize that you will have to force yourself through the movement you have. But despite all this, someone who is deceptive will continue to do so without even thinking twice.

There are a number of caveats that have been linked to this type of indicator. First of all, this type of indicator is not applicable to a short sentence or a one-word answer. Instead, it is only suitable in a narrative response. For example, consider that a human head might make a quick nod when a person says "No." This is just a simple emphasis and not a disconnect. Second, it is also very important not to forget that a nod does not necessarily mean "Yes" in certain cultures. In such cultures, even a side-to-side head movement does not imply that the person is saying "No."

Deceptive people always hide their eyes or mouth when they are not telling the truth. There is a tendency to want to cover up a given lie, so if a person's hand moves in front of their mouth while they're answering a certain question, that becomes meaningful.

In such a case, hiding one's eyes may be an inclination to protect a person from the survival of those to whom he may lie. If an individual shields or covers their eyes when answering a question, what they may also show, at the subconscious level, is that they cannot bear to see the reaction to the lie they are telling. In most cases, this type of eye protection could be done using the hand, or the person could also decide to close their eyes. Blinking is not pictured here, but when a person closes their eyes while answering a question that doesn't need reflection to answer, which can be seen as a way to hide their eyes, thus becoming a possible deceptive indicator.

Swallowing or throat clearing

If a person noisily swallows saliva or clears their throat before answering a certain question, then there is a problem somewhere. However, if any of these actions are performed after they have answered the question, there is nothing to worry about. But when it happens before answering a question, then there are some things that should be analyzed.

The person could make the non-verbal equivalent of the following verbal statements: "I swear to God ..." This is one of the ways to dress the lie in the best way before presenting it. Looking at it from a physiological point of view, the question may have created a type of anxiety spike, which can in addition cause dryness and discomfort in the throat and mouth.

The other way to determine if someone is telling a lie is to check what they are doing with their faces or in the head region whenever a question is asked. Usually, this would take the form of licking or biting the lips or even pulling the ears or lips together. The main reason behind this reflects one of the simple scientific questions that are usually discussed in high school. When you have a question to someone and notice that it creates a kind of anxiety spike, what you should remember is that the right answer will be harmful. In return, this will activate the autonomic nervous system to get to work and try to dissipate anxiety, which may appear to be draining a lot of blood from the surface of the extremities, ears, and face. The effects of this could be an itchy or cold sensation. Without the person noticing, their hands will be attracted to the mentioned areas and hand rubbing or twisting may occur. And that's right, you may have spotted a deceptive indicator.

The touch of the nose

Women usually perform this special gesture with smaller strokes than those of men, to avoid smudging their makeup. One of the most important things to remember is that this type of action should be read in context and in groups, as the person could have any cold or fever.

According to a group of scientists at the Chicago-based Smell & Taste Treatment and Research Foundation, when someone lies, chemicals called catecholamines are released that cause the tissue inside the nose to swell. Scientists have applied a special imaging camera that reveals blood flow in the body and shows that deliberately lying can also lead to an increase in blood pressure. This technology shows that the human nose tends to expand with blood when someone lies, and this is what is called the Pinocchio effect.

The maximized blood pressure will also swell the nose and make the nose tingle nervous, leading to a kind of brisk rubbing with the hand to suppress the itchy effect.

The swelling cannot be seen with naked eyes, but is usually what causes the nose touch gesture. The same phenomenon will also occur when a person is angry, anxious and upset. American psychiatrist Charles Wolf and neurologist Alan Hirsch carried out a detailed analysis of Bill Clinton's Grand Jury testimony about his relationship with Monica Lewinsky. They realized that whenever he was honest, he rarely touched his nose. However, when he lied, he offered that he appeared to have a frown before giving the answer and touched his nose once every 4 minutes for a total of 26 nose touches. Scientists also said that the former US president did not touch his nose at all when he offered the answers to the questions truthfully.

A deliberate action of scratching or rubbing, as opposed to a nose that may just itch slightly, usually satisfies someone's itchy nose. Usually, an itch is a repetitive and isolated signal and is out of context or inconsistent with the person's overall conversation.

When a child doesn't want to see something, the only thing they will do is cover their eyes. They usually do this with both hands. On the other hand, when an adult does not want to see something unpleasant for him, he is likely to rub his eyes. The eye is one of the brain's attempts to block out a doubt, deception or anything in bad taste it sees. It is also done to avoid facing the person being told the lie. Usually, men rub their eyes firmly and may look away if the myth is true madness.

Women are unlikely to use the eye rubbing gesture. Instead, they'll use sweet and small touching emotions just under the eyes as they either want to avoid interfering with the makeup they wear, or they've been redesigned as girls to avoid making different gestures. Sometimes, they may also want to avoid the listener's gaze by trying to look away.

One of the commonly used phrases out there is lying through the teeth. It is used to refer to a group of gestures that portray false smiles and clenched teeth, accompanied by the famous eye rubbing. It is a common gesture used by film actors to show some level of dishonesty and by other traditions such as English, who will prefer not to say what exactly they are thinking.

Chapter 12 How to identify the romantic interest?

Finding the right romantic partner, for both women and men, requires careful analysis and evaluation of your options. While it's sometimes hard to know for sure if someone has a romantic interest in you, being sure will make it easier for you to determine your next move. Whether the person in question is a casual acquaintance or a longtime friend, paying attention to the telltale signs of a romantic attraction is the first step in getting close to you or them making a move and revealing their true feelings.

To assess the feasibility of a romantic interest, do the following:

First, consider the amount of eye contact the other party gives you. The number of times and the intensity will reveal whether the person has developed romantic feelings for you. Actions will also give you a clue. For example, does he or she scan your entire body during your interactions, or does he keep glancing at you throughout the day? If he does, it means that you have become the object of his romantic thoughts.

The second step is to examine the individual's body in the course of your interactions. Realize that although verbal communication is essential, non-verbal communication is a critical element in indicating an attraction. Some of the confirmatory signs you will see include the person looking for opportunities to touch your skin or the person who comes closest when you speak to them in an attempt to catch every word you say. The person may even begin to mirror what you do, which should tell you that they are available to relate to you on a personal level.

The third thing you do is evaluate the amount of attention the person is giving you. Pay attention to how the person reacts when you talk about your personal life. For example, he will be visibly angry when you talk about the good times you had with someone else, or he may seek more information about your interests, hobbies, and goals in life. If the man is equally willing to talk to you about himself, his interests, what he intends to do with his life, his goals and ambitions, then you should rest assured that he is interested in you. The man will also enjoy engaging in topics that stimulate reflection with you.

The fourth thing you should do is pay attention to the efforts the individual puts into his desire to please you. Actions like this can range from simple things like pulling out a chair for you to sit on, to amazing acts like changing her entire wardrobe to accommodate a lazy comment you made, perhaps about how you like to dress your man.

You should also keep track of the compliments the new interest pays you because they will reveal to you what you are like in his eyes. For example, she might say that you seem to be a good mother or wife, which means she sees the potential in you to become a wife and mother, which she greatly admires.

Signs that a man has a romantic interest in you
The section above approached romantic interest from a general perspective, but used the pronoun "he". Based on that reading, you already have an idea of how men express their interest.

This section briefly points out some other signs that indicate that a man is interested in a woman:

Getting jealous easily

If her romantic interest has another guy around her or she's flirting with another guy, she quickly gets offended. The girl may not yet be his, but she's definitely working on it.

Tell the woman he wants her

If a man tells a woman he is interested in her, he is. It's the most obvious way he can communicate his interest. If he could put it into words, it must be true.

Listening to what he has to say

A guy who wants a woman will make every effort to hear everything he has to say. He'll also appear interested in things he would normally never be surprised to do like talking about the latest celebrity couple, discussing recipes, and other things guys usually don't care about.

I can't take my eyes off her

The man is hypnotized by the woman and, for this reason, is unable to keep his eyes away from her. Watching her, he is monitoring her every move and behavior, trying to find out more about her. On the other hand, she will be on the lookout for other potential men who would have their eyes on his chosen woman.

Improve its appearance

When a guy studies what his potential woman likes, he'll change different aspects of himself to appear attractive to her. First on his agenda will be his appearance. He will change his wardrobe, go for a better haircut and maintain good hygiene to make sure he catches the lady's attention. When a man is willing to move this far, he is definitely interested.

Enlist the help of friends to arrange an appointment
When a guy starts introducing a girl to his friends, he does so hoping she'll hang around for a while. It's also a way to mark his territory to ensure his friends won't start chasing you.

Personal space doesn't matter anymore

Guys will choose body language every day rather than gushing you with their words. Even though a guy like this will tell you what you want to hear, his top priority is body language. A guy who likes you will invade your personal space by getting closer to the distance between you two to touch you.

Is present

A man will not spend time with a woman unless he is a good friend of his or wants her. Once he's interested, he'll find all sorts of excuses to spend some time with her. He may also give up the time he spends with his male friends to be with her. Identify the romantic interest in a woman

It's hard to tell if a friend you've known for a long time or even just recently would like to take your friendship to the next level.

Traditionally, men are the ones who make the first move, push their date to give that first kiss, and make an effort to initiate higher levels of intimacy with women. All this responsibility can put pressure on a man making it difficult for him to make the first move. However, research shows that women are the ones who signal whether the man can go ahead and initiate the whole love process or not.

Having understood this, what non-verbal cues do women point to to let the other person know that they have developed a romantic interest?

Body language
If this is a friend you have known for a long time, try to see if he hugs you tightly or if he hugs you with one hand like you are unwanted. If a woman is interested in you, she will pamper and hug you for longer. She will spend an unusual amount of time looking into your eyes and when you meet her on the street or in the hallways, she will show you that secret smile.

Suppose he has developed a romantic interest in a stranger in a restaurant, classroom or any other place where a love interest would develop, his behavior changes slightly compared to when dealing with a friend. His secret weapon will be his gaze.

The woman will keep an extended gaze on the man she deems attractive and will keep it until the man notices her. When he does, she will smile, break her gaze, look back at him, smile again, and then break her gaze again. (That's a lot, I know).

Another strategy he will use is to pimp. She'll go two extra miles to look good in preparation for meeting the man she has an interest in. She will fix her hair, assume an open body posture (where the arms are kept away from the body) or orient her body towards the man.

Once the man approaches her, which most men always do, both sides orient their bodies towards each other and the woman can continue to engage in her seductive behavior such as touching herself, palming (opening the palm and wrist and showing them) and leaning back to expose his neck.

If you suspect that your friend, perhaps one you've known for a long time, is showing the body language signs discussed, the next time you meet her, suddenly grab her and pull her towards you. Bring her so close that you can feel how her body reacts, such as a rapid heartbeat or increased breathing. If she stays there and doesn't snap away, and her pupils dilate in anticipation of her next move, lean down and kiss her.

Its time

A woman interested in you will do anything to make time for you no matter how tight her schedule is. Maybe he recently started apologizing for meeting you every other day. If she really did, this confirms that she is interested in pursuing a romantic relationship with you.

A woman will continually try to spend more time with a man she likes. For example, if she chooses to spend Friday night with you instead of accompanying her friends, she definitely likes you.

Joins and appreciates your company

You should know that a woman likes you if she shows signs that she enjoys your company immensely. He will laugh heartily at your jokes, even at the dry ones. When he feels down, you are the first person he will call. This is also what he will do when he is excited about something. Whenever she feels like she has been mistreated, she will call you to complain, possibly suggesting that she sees you as a source of safety, both emotionally and physically. When you finish the conversation, she will be cheerful again and her spirits will have lifted.

A lady will ask you to accompany her to public places such as social events, because she wants to flaunt you to other people, introduce you to her family if you haven't met them already, and take pictures with you. Whenever you spend time with her, time seems to fly by and she keeps asking you to come back one more time.

Jealousy
Jealousy is one of the protective tools a woman has towards the man she has aroused an interest in. Surprisingly, a woman will be attracted to a man who already has a woman in his arms but won't want to share it once he has it. A woman who wants you for herself will ask you to treat her differently and especially by how you treat other women in your life. If you show interest in another woman or hold a hand, the girl inside you will sulk all day, block your calls, and won't talk to you until you agree with your mistake and apologize.

If you hang out with your friends and a lady sitting across from you likes you, notice how your eyes will lock every time. If she's sitting next to a guy, she'll want to hold him tighter to see how you react, whether you're jealous or not.

He confides in you

Once a lady has appreciated you, she will tell you all kinds of intimate details about herself and the issues surrounding her work and family. It will also make you understand his fears. He will try to know your opinion on various issues, from how his character comes out, his clothing, politics, his career, to the state of the economy. Over time, the two of you will connect so well that your conversations will sound like heart-to-heart murmurs.

See how his friends treat you

The way the girl's close friends treat you should make you understand how she feels about you. If you go out and then apologize for giving you some quiet time, or between conversations they joke that you two would make a nice couple, know that she absolutely likes you.

Conversely, if they act bored every time you are around, apologize or ignore you altogether, know that it means nothing to their friend. Some will even be bold enough to let you know the truth, in the face. In a case like this, run to save yourself and don't look back.

He considers you special

A woman who likes you from time to time will bend some of her principles and rules to fit you. He would never do these things for other men. For example, she will spend the days that are important to her with you. He will stay by your side taking care of you when you get the flu. It will leave clues in your home like a toothbrush or piece of clothing. It will also wear your perfume. All this he will do in the hope that you see him and somehow reciprocate the special treatment.

Try to get a better version of yourself

Once a woman has confirmed your eligibility as her mate, she starts working to help you become your ideal self. For example, it will begin to convince you of your self-destructive habits such as excessive alcohol intake, clutter, or skipping classes. It will urge you to become more responsible, clean your home, and take your studies or work more seriously. He will suggest you a haircut that will enhance your look.

Overall, a woman who likes you will want to help you become a better man because she imagines you will be her husband.

Signs that you have developed a romantic interest
Starting to love someone is different for everyone. Some people recognize the sensation immediately, while others are not so sure about it, or consider it infatuation. Either way, however, your body will step in and let you know if the sensation is leaving you with some not-so-subtle marks that you like someone. These signs include: I can't stop staring at the person

Eye contact is a sign that you are fixated on something. Therefore, if you can't stop staring at someone, he or she is your fixation.

Get a "high" feel

When you are interested in someone, it is natural to feel like you are out of your mind. One study found that when you like someone, your brain behaves like when you're high on cocaine. This should explain your "high" feeling.

Always thinking about that person

When you like someone romantically, it's hard to get them off your mind. The brain releases a chemical called phenylethylamine, which gives you the feeling of infatuation.

Having a desire to make the person happy

Appreciating someone makes you want to live in their world. Their happiness becomes yours, as do sad times. Since happiness is the desired emotion, you will want to do whatever it takes to make that person happy, even at the expense of your own happiness.

The pain is not that intense

Interestingly, once you fall in love with someone, a literal fall won't feel that pain. One study confirmed that interest and love reduce the pain felt, by about 40% to 15%.

Suddenly becoming open to new experiences

Everyone wants to impress someone they like, but if you find yourself wanting to try things the other person likes, you are genuinely impressed.

Creepy things don't bother you anymore
If you're an extreme germ phobo, suddenly it's okay to kiss your partner knowing he hasn't brushed his teeth in days. A study confirmed that feelings of love and sexual interest outweigh all gross feelings.

Sweat more

When you've fallen in love with someone, you tend to exhibit physical symptoms of illness such as excessive sweating, anxiety, stress, and an upset stomach. Therefore, the next time you feel unwell, check that you are not in love.

Oddities turn you on

Chances are you like the things that make the person unique, which perhaps attracted you to them. One study found that quirks cause people to fall more deeply in love with physical appearance as well.

Chapter 13 How to determine personality types?

Clearly understanding what type of personality people fit into will make it easy for you to better analyze people. Here are the characteristics that will help you understand the four main dimensions of personalities which are Perception Vs Intuition and Thinking Vs Feeling.

Perception characteristics include practical, specific, is based on numbers and facts, lives in the moment and cares about ongoing problems. Intuitive people, on the other hand, are inspirational and insightful, rely on trends, theories and insights to draw conclusions, and are future-oriented.

Characteristics of thinking include rationality, reasoning, impersonal, cold, objective, and the use of objective methods and logical analysis to make decisions and solve problems. Characteristics of feeling include being governed by feelings and emotions, showing sympathy, concern and support, and making decisions based on gut feeling.

You will need to combine the personality dimensions above with two other dichotomous dimensions including introversion and extroversion to arrive at an accurate personality type analysis. So, here are some characteristics of extroverts and introverts as defined by Carl Jung.

Characteristics of extroverts

According to this psychologist, extroversion refers to a personality's tendency towards action-oriented jobs as a response to everything that happens around him or her. For extroverts, active actions are the first response call to all information and events in the world and the surrounding environment.

These people draw energy and motivation from the outside world. They have great networking skills and have a large number of contacts on their list despite their personal and professional life not requiring this social connection. Positive characteristics of extroverts include being talkative, action-oriented, outgoing, friendly, enthusiastic, and outgoing. Negative characteristics of extroverts included attention seeking, very easy distraction, and their inability to spend time with themselves.

Here are five important personality traits of extroverts:

Extroverts love to talk- Known as talkers many times, extroverts love to talk to everyone, including co-workers, family and friends. They also like to just start a conversation with complete strangers. Meeting new people and getting to know them through conversation is their greatest passion. Extroverts have a large social network and enjoy the company of people. It is very easy for extroverts to make friends.

Extroverts feel inspired and energized by social interactions- Socialization loads the body and mind. After spending time with people and talking and enjoying their company, extroverts don't get tired. On the contrary, they feel energized and inspired to do more. For them, socializing is a very refreshing and rejuvenating activity, and their energy level drops if they are left alone for a long time. If the choice is between spending time with people and spending time alone, then you know what choice the extrovert will make.

They solve problems through discussions- Extroverts prefer to discuss problems and issues and solve them rather than internalize them and find solutions on their own. Talking about the problem helps extroverts gain a thorough understanding of the problem and thus they can easily strategize on the best solution. Extroverts love to talk about their day at the office or school because this helps them release stress and eliminate the pressures they felt during the day.

Extroverts are generally known for being helpful and friendly- Since extroverts love to interact with people, they are usually known to be very helpful and friendly. During a social gathering, an extrovert will be the first person to go up and greet a new guest and make the necessary introductions. Being seen as helpful and friendly makes it very easy for extroverts to socialize with people and make new friends.

Extroverts are generally very open in their interactions and it is very easy to understand them - Extroverts like to openly share their thoughts with others and it is very easy to understand them because they will tell you exactly how they feel.

Some generalized characteristics of extroverts include:

- Wide range of interests

- Likes to communicate through conversations and conversations

- Love being the center of attraction

- Quite impulsive and tends to act first and then think

- Likes to work in a team

- He feels isolated if left alone for a long time

- See the outside world to recharge your batteries with energy and for inspiration and motivation

- Likes to talk openly about feelings and thoughts

Characteristics of introverts

Introversion is a tendency of the personality to look inside one's thoughts, feelings and perceptions to find answers to questions. Introverts derive energy and sustenance from spending time alone and use their inner world to stimulate innovation and new ideas. They won't have a very large social circle and taking on jobs that require them to meet new people can be a difficult situation for them. Here are some personality traits of introverts:

Surrounded by many people, it drains energy- Introverts feel exhausted from excessive socialization. They need to take some time on their own after spending time with people to recover their drained energy and feel recharged. Introverts consume energy during interactions with people and charge up when alone compared to extroverts who gain energy during social interactions and feel drained when alone.

Introverts love solitude- Introverts love to spend their free time alone with their personal passions and hobbies. Reading a book alone on a quiet Saturday afternoon will rejuvenate an introvert like nothing else. However, you need to remember that enjoying solitude doesn't mean introverts always want to be alone. Many introverts enjoy spending quality time with family and friends. Their time alone is a time to recharge and they love being with themselves.

Introverts usually have a very small group of close friends- Introverts like to be with people. But usually, their group of friends forms a small, small group of friends. They don't like having a large circle of friends and social connections. They don't like wasting time and energy on a large group of people they have only a superficial relationship with. They prefer to use that time and energy to spend a meaningful time with close friends with whom they share a deeper relationship.

Introverts are generally described as quiet people and it's not easy to understand them- Introverts are seen as reserved, quiet, calm and sometimes even shy people. While some people may be very shy, you shouldn't mistake their privacy for shyness. They will find the determination to react when actually needed. They just don't like to waste energy on unnecessary conversations and will instead choose their words carefully. For this reason, introverts appear calm and not easy to understand and know.

Excessive external stimulation distracts introverts- Frantic activities and excessive external stimuli can distract introverts and make them uncomfortable. Introverts feel overwhelmed by hectic social conditions and prefer quieter environments.

Introverts are self-aware- Introverts spend a lot of time analyzing and thinking about their experiences and responses to various situations. This makes them very aware of themselves and their inner world. They just love to sit down, analyze and reflect on things so that their self-awareness improves.

Introverts are excellent observers- Unlike extroverts who like to dive and swim upstream, introverts first like to learn a lot through observation and then make an informed decision. First they think and then act against extroverts who first act and then think. If introverts have to take on a particular task, they would first like to observe a master doing it and analyze each move and understand if it is possible to replicate it. Only when they are absolutely certain will they start working alone. They love to learn through observation.

Introverts love tasks that allow them independence - Introverts like to work alone and are quite wary of having too many social interactions at work. Therefore, they love any job that allows them independence and freedom to work alone and alone. An introvert can be a great writer, accountant, graphic designer, computer programmer, artist, etc. Where working alone is the norm rather than the exception.

Introverts do not suffer from social anxiety or shyness- Introverts love to be with themselves. However, they do not suffer from any kind of mental problem such as shyness or social anxiety. They can easily converse with strangers too. They may not take the first step, but once they get started they are able to carry the conversation forward without any problems or hitches.

The most important thing to remember is that there is no black and white range for extroverts and introverts. There are no perfect extroverts and introverts either. Most people share the characteristics of both types. However, one particular type is usually more dominant than the other. And one type is no better than the other in any way. There are strengths and weaknesses to both personality traits.

As you analyze people, you should be able to easily discern traits and then use them to understand why they do what they do without being judgmental or temperamental about anything. Most theories reveal that nearly all people in the world are neither completely introverted nor completely extroverted. Most of us are in the middle of the scale.

Using the above information and through careful observation, it is possible to analyze people by being aware of their personality types. Once you get their personality type more or less correctly, predicting their behaviors in a given scenario will become easier than otherwise allowing you to be in a position of strength and power.

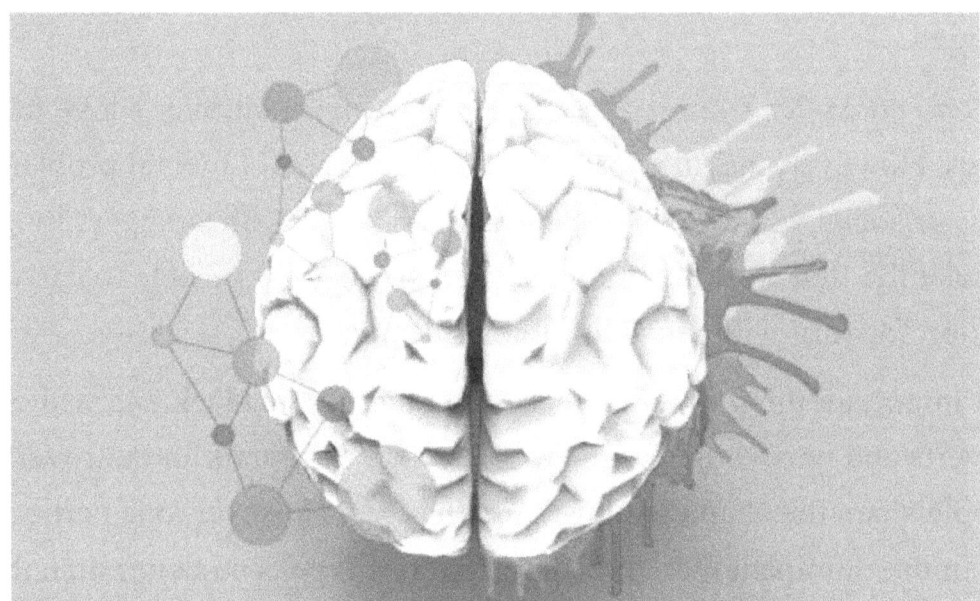

Chapter 14 Analysis of verbal communication

A conscious effort has been made to analyze non-verbal ways of communicating, but then there is a lot to learn from the people who speak too. I mentioned something about the word, in fact, but then, as the most important way of communication, it is crucial that I treat verbal communication as a chapter.

That said, you can't expect people to tell you about their deepest concerns or character flaws. However, we can learn a lot by learning to listen and knowing when to speak. Learning to listen beyond the surface is a key part of verbal communication. In order for you to do a good analysis on a person, you need to make sure you overcome prejudices when you listen to them, as this will affect your mind and the truth.

This is simply a quality of a person's voice that can be used to determine what others think of them. The general belief is that women always have a higher pitched voice, while men always have lower tones. Beyond gender differences, however, low voices have been linked to calm, reassurance and a reassuring disposition. This is the real reason why hospitals, call centers, and customer support services prefer agents with relatively low voices.

The tone of our voice can be controlled in four different ways; chest, nose, mouth and diaphragm. People who speak with their noses will sound whiny and shrill; people who speak with their mouths have lower tones than they do. When you notice someone speaking in a higher tone than normal, it can mean agitation, excitement or panic.

Most people speak from the chest, and this is to ensure they are heard. But then, it can become tiring later on and the speaker will have no choice but to speak in a harsh voice. However, the best place to speak from is the diaphragm. The diaphragm is strong, full and requires a lot of training before it can be used effectively. It's also great if you want to speak in a tone that communicates calm and authority.

Speech patterns

The pattern of speech is simply the way people speak; it's basically how fast the speech is and the pauses that are taken around the flow. For example, being too quick with your speech makes you sound rushed and can be interpreted as a meaning of anxiety. What people will think is that you are probably just pouring out everything that comes to your mind without even thinking deeply about what is coming out of your mouth. As you try to analyze people, keep in mind that most fast speakers are likely nervous. Many people cannot stop talking quickly when they are nervous or anxious.

On the other hand, people who speak with slow, measured pauses sound authoritative, calm, and friendly. The way they speak indicates that they are taking the time to think about what they have to say before saying it. However, it is important to mention that this can sometimes be tricky because if your speech is too slow, it could indicate that you are distracted or possibly tired. Your audience may get bored if they observe that your speech lacks enthusiasm. Realize that speaking slowly can be helpful in gaining more room for thoughts. However, overly confused language can be a harbinger of boredom.

Fillers and pronouns

Does the person you're talking to use a lot of filler words? What is your use of the pronoun? Does it stop a lot and is filled with useless words?

Fillers are words that interrupt the normal voice flow without adding any specific meaning to the overall message. Examples of fillers include "like", "um", "uh", "err" and the like. All fillers have been considered bad lately, and generally speaking, the advice is that people avoid them and eliminate them completely.

For example, the repetition of "um" by a speaker indicates a certain level of insecurity or anxiety. Most of the time, people use fillers when they have memorized information with certain pointers. In an effort to remember these tips, fillers are introduced in place of the long, uncomfortable pauses.

How a person uses pronouns can provide another fascinating insight into their current state of mind. In particular, how a person employs and uses "You", "I" and "we" can provide instructive discourse. Usually, when "I" is used to convey instructions, it is a message of authority. "I" also provides a dominant and intimidating atmosphere in these cases. "I" is a strong choice of words, especially when the person speaking to you is your supervisor at work or an older family member. It connotes and denotes a powerful desire when used to request it.

On the other hand, "We" is the safest option people use when they need to do a task, they find unpleasant. "We" could also be used to mitigate the potential impact of news about to be delivered. For example, it's easier to hide behind "We" when firing someone. It's always "We can't keep hiring you", instead of using "I". It can also be a way to escape responsibility for a wrongdoing or unpleasant task. In short, "we" is very useful when you want to communicate that a situation is out of your control. However, when "We" does not refer to a single entity or organization, it can be an indicator of "union", especially in unheated situations.

Using "You" is particularly complex. It all depends on the context and tone of the speaker. "You" can seem accusatory in the right situations. A speaker who emphasizes "You" might try to convey a non-engagement or non-consent message. "You", however, may also seem soothing. However, more often than not, "You" is a dissociation message; people frequently use it in conversation to make it clear that they are a separate entity from the other side. Learn to notice when "You" is accusatory. Match its use with other visual cues like frown or frown.

Chapter 15 The Type of Skill No Communication

Communication seems like it should be a fairly straightforward process. However, nothing could be further from the truth. It's not just about interpreting and understanding what someone is trying to tell you in their words. It is also about all the other dynamics that are happening, what else the person is saying with their body, if their verbal message is something that should be taken literally, or if there is something more that needs to be considered. . This is the key to learning to analyze people because you are now trying to decipher their hidden meaning. Trying to find out what they're not necessarily telling you right now.

Verbal versus non-verbal

When a person uses language and sound to convey their messages and intentions, it is a form of verbal communication. Verbal communication is defined as a channel through which people use to express their ideas, concepts and desires. This form of communication is extremely crucial in many contexts, including work, home and daily life. It is how we teach and how we learn, and we use this form of communication more than any other in our daily survival.

The written word is also associated with the act of verbal communication. When we read the words before us, we mentally repeat them to ourselves in our mind. Sometimes, we can even say it out loud. Verbal communication, therefore, involves both sound and the written word. Words are the form of communication that humans have used to exchange their thoughts and messages, especially when they are not in a face-to-face context.

An example of verbal communication involves speaking in public. This is where communication is conducted and conducted verbally to audience groups. Another is interpersonal communication, which involves a group of people who can listen and speak at the same time. Other examples of verbal communication include the daily conversations with your friends, family, colleagues, clients, and even random strangers that you meet throughout your day.

Verbal communication is important because it is our primary way of conveying our messages. We rely on this method of communication to:

- Inform, investigate, discuss, discuss and disseminate information and ideas.
- Teach others and learn from them
- Tie and build relationships
- Get the results you want
- Work together as a team or group with others to achieve a common goal

Non-verbal communication, on the other hand, relies on other forms of communication that do not involve the use of words or sounds. This is the category that body language falls into. When we use gestures, body movements and facial expressions to convey our intent, which is a form of non-verbal communication. Is non-verbal communication as important as verbal communication? Yes, it does. Maybe even more.

It can't be stressed enough how important it is to make a good first impression. An example of where first impressions are absolutely critical is during a job interview. From the moment you walk into the room and even before you say your first word, you communicate with your employer in a non-verbal way. Your posture, facial expression, and even the gestures you make will be the clues your employer is looking for when evaluating you. The same thing happens when you conduct important business or meet with clients. The impression you leave on people can be a big deciding factor in determining the outcome of your success. Saying all the right words, but with the wrong body language, won't give you the desired results you seek.

What you see versus what you hear

From the moment you meet someone for the first time, they leave an impression on you. What kind of impression depends on what they convey with their body language? Learning to analyze someone means matching what you see and hear currently in the social environment you are in, and then probably draw your own conclusions. The human brain tends to see only what we want to see, and now you must learn to cross those boundaries if you truly want to learn the hidden messages that a person transmits with their subtle body signals and movements.

To what extent do you think you are able to spot the contradictory messages right now? Body language is such a fascinating subject. It's like unraveling a puzzle as you search for hidden clues and meanings of what you see and hear. Politicians are a good place to start practicing your body analysis skills. Politicians are fascinating because there are some who have been guilty of saying they believe in something that isn't necessarily true. They often pretend to be someone they are not. As a result, these people spend a lot of their time trying to dodge awkward questions, lying, pretending, and faking the public in order to survive.

Types of non-verbal communication

Communication is the general concept. To be effective, you need to be able to communicate clearly in both your words and body language. In fact, the two should be in sync with each other, because that's when you send some of your most powerful messages to the recipient, combining the power of the spoken word with the equally formidable power of body language.

Some examples of the ways we communicate non-verbal include:

- Facial expressions - This is responsible for much of what we communicate non-verbal. A smile or a frown can be more powerful than multiple words combined. Since your face is often the first part of you that people will notice, even before they hear what you have to say, your facial expressions are your strongest non-verbal point of contact.
- Gesture - The deliberate signals and movements we use when we speak are also a form of non-verbal communication. Shaking, pointing and using fingers as a quantity of numerical indicators are all ways in whichwe communicate with the absence of words. A perfect example of how

powerful gestures can be is in a courtroom, where lawyers are well known for relying on different methods and techniques of non-verbal communication in an effort to influence opinions to win their case.

- Posture - Body language also involves the posture you present. Someone who feels confident, for example, is tall, straight, and proud to silently communicate to the rest of the world that they feel secure. Someone who is clumsy, shy, and clumsy, on the other hand, communicates this through hunched shoulders and arms crossed across their chest.

- Proximity - Proximity to someone (and vice versa) is also a form of non-verbal communication. Proximity might vary between cultures, and when someone doesn't feel comfortable being too close to you, there will be body language cues to look out for. This includes avoiding eye contact, folding your arms across your chest, tapping your fingers or toes, and visibly walking a step or two away from you.

- Paralinguistic Communication - Now, these include all other aspects of non-verbal communication aside from body movements and facial expressions. Paralinguistics refers to the inflection of the voice, pitch, pitch, timbre and rhythm of your voice. These fall under non-verbal communication, even if it ties back into speech because it involves the underlying aspects of what a person is saying. The tone of voice they use, for example, could have a very different meaning from the words they pronounce. When a person says I'm fine but in a short, cutting tone that brings with it a hint of anger, this is a significant clue that the person is, in fact, not well at all.

- Touch - One of the most used forms of non-verbal communication is the element of touch. Touch is a powerful move or gesture that is capable of conveying a wide range of emotional messages that a person may want to communicate with you. A warm hug, for example, indicates that the person is happy to see you or happy to have you around. Or thatthey look after you and are happy to see you after a long time. A quick, short hug, on the other hand, communicates that the person is likely uncomfortable with the gesture, the situation, or that the person is uncomfortable around you.

- Locomotion - The amount of movement that occurs during a communication process is a clear indicator of how busy that person is. Let's say the person you were talking to is constantly on the move, fidgeting, walking up and down or just gesturing too much, inhibiting the opportunity for effective communication.

Why non-verbal communication is important

Non-verbal communication is a powerful element and, therefore, it has several advantages in its name that make it stand out more than verbal communication. When used in conjunction with verbal communication, it can lead to effective communication and relationship building sessions. By itself, non-verbal communication is still a powerful force to contend with.

The ability to analyze others based on their non-verbal communication, therefore, is an important skill because:

- It helps you uncover the hidden meaning the speaker is conveying, so you can tailor your responses appropriately to the situation and cultivate the desired outcome.

- Being able to accurately assess and analyze another person's body language improves your empathy and social skills (which therefore improves your emotional intelligence levels). By learning to identify facial cues and body movements, you will be able to reach levels of communication that others are not, simply because you can see what others cannot.

- It is a clue to provide valuable information on what the speaker is not saying in his or her words.

- It is used to express emotions and empathy in a powerful way.

- Increase your understanding of the messages you receive.

When used in tandem with verbal communication, both of these the elements combined can provide a deeper and more meaningful insight into the speaker's message.

- Being able to interpret these non-verbal cues effectively is how you get the upper hand over the other person. Misinterpretations can often lead to disastrous effects, so why not try analyzing body language thoroughly instead?

- Help strengthen your relationships. People tend to feel a connection with those they believe can "understand" them in a way that others cannot. Being able to analyze body language gives you this ability because you can see clues to what is really going on, even when the other person thinks they haven't said a word about it.• The right gestures and expressions can be a good substitute when you don't know the right words to say. Hugging your friend or family member with a close, loving hug can communicate your love and support more powerfully than words.

- It can be used to reinforce messages if used in the right way. When you give someone directions, for example, pointing out the right path to take strengthens their understanding of what you are trying to tell them.

Our non-verbal communication signals are just as important - one could even say of equal importance - for both our verbal and written communication. One cannot exist without the other. To thoroughly analyze other people, start by recognizing the importance of both of these forms of communication, not only in others, but in yourself as well. What messages are you conveying with your body language?

Non-verbal cues that convey confidence at work

By now you have a pretty clear idea of the non-verbal cues you need to look for that reveal hidden clues about a person's true desire and intention. But what about the type of messages you are communicating with your body language?

What can you do to give the right non-verbal signals, especially if you want to achieve success in an environment like your workplace? As important as it is to be able to read and analyze others, we need to make sure we are also giving the right messages. In case someone is analyzing you (and you can be sure there will be at least one or two people reading your clues).

Part of what makes successful people so, well, successful is the fact that they know how to use verbal and non-verbal communication to their advantage. Especially non-verbal communication, which they know can send the strongest messages of all. If you notice, successful people often stand tall, straight, and with an air of confidence. They smile, make eye contact and move with intent and purpose. They use carefully chosen gestures during speeches, gestures that have been specifically selected to emphasize the impact of their words to project their messages in the most effective way.

These individuals know how important non-verbal communication is and they also know how to position themselves in relation to the people around them. They avoid getting too close because they understand it could be perceived as threatening or overwhelming. They also avoid staying too far away because they know they might be sending the wrong message, that they feel distant when that might not be the case. They know how to read their surroundings and anticipate what move another person might make. They made sure they understood these skills so well that it allowed them to be successful in their careers.

If you want to start excelling in your career, then effective body language is where you start building your foundation. If there has ever been a place where non-verbal communication skills matter most, it's in the workplace. This is where you are most observed, especially by your managers and superiors. The most successful people who eventually become leaders and managers in the workplace are the ones who are able to make a great impression on everyone they work with because of the way they communicate. You can be the best at your job in any way possible, but if you don't leave a positive impression on the people around you, your knowledge and skills will only carry you so far.

Being confident is an important part of becoming an effective communicator overall. As busy as you are analyzing the body language of the people around you, there will surely be at least one or two other people who are analyzing you.

It's not just the body language of others that matters. Your body language is also important.

When you interact with others around you in the workplace, the moment you demonstrate that you are confident, you will find it much easier to have effective conversations with your colleagues and team members who will get things done. Because? Because they are drawn to your confident approach. Self-confident people are not hindered by challenges, they stand up to face them and this is what people at work want to follow. Someone who knows what he is doing and is doing it with confidence.

Remember how our non-verbal signals make the most powerful messages of all resonate without saying a word? This is the body language for you. Body language is applicable in the workplace too, perhaps even more so because that's where it really matters. At work, the way you behave and communicate is just as important as how you get the job done. To convey trust non-verbal, you need to start by adopting confident body language every time you walk into your workplace. Don't bend over, don't fold or cross your arms, and don't frown or look grumpy. Always be positive and project a warm and welcoming way. Smile and look people you meet in the eye.

Other ways you can project confidence with your body include:

- Power Poses - Social psychologist Amy Cuddy, during her TED Talk in 2012, revealed that power poses can be effective when it comes to looking and feeling more confident. An example of a safe power pose here involves opening your body and positioning it in such a way that it appears to take up more "space". Think about the greater term of life. Inflate your chest out, roll your shoulders back and avoid bending over as if you're trying to hide from the world.

- Observe hand gestures - All it takes is that the wrong gestures are used to completely convey the wrong message. To beobserving hand gestures is important to represent trust in a non-verbal way at work. You need to be able to achieve this without the use of hand gestures that could be misinterpreted in the wrong way. When explaining an idea, for example, keep your palms open and your fingers together. This is a universal gesture that communicates openness, trust, cooperation and acceptance.

- Maintain eye contact - Maintaining eye contact is one of the foundational rules for effective non-verbal communication. When you engage in eye contact with the person you are talking to, you are effectively showing them that you are interested and eager to hear what they have to say.

- Be aware of your "space" - Ideally, you should respect an individual's personal space when communicating with him. Special awareness is as much a part of the non-verbal communication process as facial expressions and body posture. Pay close attention to the person you are talking to and watch for signs of discomfort, especially if you are in the office. The moment you notice that they are not comfortable with your proximity; take a few steps back to create a comfortable enough space between the two of you.

- Handshakes can be more revealing than you think - you only get one chance to make a powerful first impression and nothing leaves a significant impact when you meet someone, especially someone new to the first handshake. Your handshake will be very revealing to the person receiving it, and just a weak, lackluster handshake is enough for that person to shut down even before the conversation has had a chance to take off. Think of your handshake as your opening line, the introduction your body is making. Firm and secure handshakes are a must to convey trust in a non-verbal way.

Chapter 16: Trust and How It Appears

Trust is a very powerful emotion in today's society. An individual who seems very confident is able to go very far. By appearing confident, a person can attract suitable mates and receive promotions based on their perceived leadership skills. For this reason, trust is very commonly shown in different ways. However, trust is also falsified many times to move forward in life. In this chapter, we'll look at the common ways that trust is shown through body language. Additionally, we will also look at how to spot a lack of trust in an individual.

Show confidence

- *Posture*

  Posture is very important in the confidence aspect. An individual's posture can tell a lot about the perceived level of confidence. Safe posture is defined by legs aligned with the individual's shoulders and feet about four to six inches apart. The weight is typically distributed equally on both legs and the shoulders are pushed back slightly. A straight back is also very typical of someone with extreme confidence. Individuals with this type of posture are considered assertive and tend to project confidence. This is because an individual with this posture is seen as being able to "stand" regardless of their height and are also perceived to be very open to those who are talking to them, as they are not afraid of any attacks or criticisms.

- *Hands*

  Hands are very important in trying to appear confident. It is important to remember when trying to show confidence with your hands to keep them calm and still. Moving your hands quickly is a sign of nervousness or anxiety.

- *Visual contact*

  Having the ability to maintain long, strong eye contact with another is a great sign that an individual is feeling confident. This is because showing eye contact with another person is a very vulnerable feeling and position. This is because our eyes can show a lot of how we actually feel in a situation. By maintaining good eye contact, we are showing the other person that we are not afraid of what they can see in our eyes. This is a sign of extreme confidence, as it shows that you are confident in your feelings and that you believe that you are not afraid of how a person will interpret what they see in your eyes.

- *Mirror your body language*

  Mirroring the body language of those around us arouses a kind of understanding and seeks acceptance from those around us. This increases our level of confidence as we humans strive to be appreciated by those around us. As those around us will subconsciously begin to appreciate us more by mirroring their body language, they will also be confident thanks to their positive view of us.

- *Get excited*

  It is very important to remember not to fidget when trying to show confidence levels. Agitating in any form, regardless of which part of the body is doing the movement, shows signs of nervousness and anxiety. Other than that, it can simply annoy those around us. People are often irritated by continuous rhythmic strokes or brushing noises. This is something to keep in mind if you are an individual who likes to bounce their leg or tap their foot in simple moments.

- A very common sign of a lack of trust in an individual is if he constantly touches the phone while in social situations or alone. If an individual finds himself unable to sit still during a social situation in which he does not know many people, this could be a sign that they lack confidence. Checking the phone is a sign that they feel awkward in a social situation and are unable to connect with those around them.

- Another sign of a lack of trust in an individual is a quick retreat during a disagreement to avoid arguing with another person. An individual with an extreme lack of trust will not want to cause trouble to a person they disagree with. For this reason, they often negotiate their views to avoid conflict. This shows that a person lacks confidence because they are unsure of their opinions and would rather back off than express themselves honestly.

- Another common sign of a lack of confidence in an individual is their inability to leave their homes without any kind of makeup or hairstyle. This is a very obvious sign of a lack of confidence because it shows that an individual does not feel that they are worth looking at unless they have something on their body or face that makes them look more beautiful. Doing makeup or styling gives a false sense of self-worth to an individual, which people with low self-esteem or confidence rely heavily on.

- An individual with little confidence will also tend to take constructive criticism too personally. If a person makes an individual constructive criticism of something, they will take it too seriously and end up experiencing very strong negative emotions. This is a huge sign of low confidence and low self-esteem because this individual is not emotionally balanced enough to handle constructive criticism from those around him.

- Individuals who have little confidence or self-esteem will also be afraid to express their opinion in conversation. They often guess themselves before saying something instead of plunging into an interesting conversation. They may find themselves stammering or breaking down. This is because these people don't know how well their views will be received and are afraid that other people will take their views negatively. This is a sign of low self-confidence eitheresteem because these individuals care a lot about how the people they come in contact with see them.

- An individual who has difficulty with trust also finds himself extremely indecisive with very simple and basic decisions. They can change their mind very often after making a decision. This is a sign of low self-esteem because this individual cannot trust their opinions or decisions. This is especially a sign of low self-confidence when it applies to very simple tasks or simple decisions.

- Individuals with low self-confidence will also have extreme difficulty handling the sincere compliments of those around them. They tend not to think they are worthy of such a good compliment and usually reject them or don't accept them.

- Individuals struggling with low self-esteem will also tend to give up very early on the things they are trying to do or achieve. They may have goals and dreams they want to fulfill, but they will give up before they even really start. This is a sign of low self-confidence because they don't believe they have the ability to realize these goals and dreams before they even begin.

- Individuals struggling with low self-esteem will also tend to confront those around them. They tend to have a very strong focus on people who are doing better than them and will point out all the ways they are not doing as well as those around them. This is a strong one
  a sign of low self-confidence because it says that the person in question does not consider themselves very successful or is doing very well in their life.

- Slouching is a very common manifestation of low self-confidence in an individual. Why so? It is because lowering the center of a person's body is a sign that a person is unwilling to support the weight of the upper body alone. It sends a signal that the individual is not proud of himself. Because of these things, this is a great sign of low self-confidence.

To detect low self-esteem in an individual, all you need to do is look for some of these common signs of low self-esteem and self-confidence. You can also detect low self-esteem or low self-esteem in yourself by looking out for these common signs. If you find that you or someone you know has low self-esteem or confidence, you can start working on it by saying very positive affirmations about yourself on a regular basis. In the next chapter, we will examine how an individual can correct their body language and how they can pretend to be more self-confident than they actually are.

Chapter 17: how to fake body language

In this chapter, we will look at some easy and simple ways to simulate your body language in order to appear as different emotions or expressions to those around you. These methods can be useful in everyday life as well as in the workplace. They can also be useful for starting a relationship for the first time. These methods also do a good job of helping you feel the way you are trying to feel. Have you ever heard the cliché: "Pretend until you make it?" Well, in some ways, this is true. By pretending to feel a lot of emotions, you may be able to convince yourself that you really feel that way.

1. Take a deep breath

By amplifying the oxygen supply in our lungs, we can receive more power and more ability to falsify our emotions through body language. This will also give us a moment to calm down and pretend to be calm and collected. Additionally, deep breathing tends to stimulate the parasympathetic nervous system, which can trigger a relaxation response. This is very good, especially when you are trying to trick people around you into believing that you are calm and in control in a situation. Deep breathing is a great trick for a conscious life, as it gives you more control over your body and your reactions to stimuli.

2. Control of the movement of our eyebrows

Our brows can convey a lot about our inner feelings. A lot of movement of our brows can convey feelings you don't want to express. You must be consciously aware of the movement of your eyebrows when you are trying to fake certain emotions through your body language.

3. Trying not to use a fake smile

While it's nice to smile even if you don't feel like it, it's not always helpful when faking your emotions through body language. While looking happy and bubbly can make others want to please you, it's not the best look to constantly have. Fake smiles are all too easy to see, and humans are naturally inclined to try and look for any inconsistencies in someone's smile. A better way to hide your emotions is to keep your mouth straight and not smile or sad.

4. Relax your face

By keeping your facial muscles relaxed, you can more easily control the movements of your face. Stay away from movements such as grinding your teeth, frowning, or showing any other type of emotional expression. Having a relaxed face and a calmer look makes it easier to better control the emotions you are conveying through body language.

5. Support your head

A person's head being held up by an individual or a face buried in a person's palm is a very obvious and clear sign of a bad mood or sadness. It's best to keep your head up and your neck and back straight in a situation where you feel sad, but you don't want those around you to know that you feel sad. Another important thing to remember is to try to stop yourself from touching your face when you are feeling sad, as it is a strong sign of anxiety and stress.

Moving suddenly or very quickly are obvious signs of discomfort and anxiety. If you try to relax your body and try to give the impression that you are comfortable where you are, then it can be easier to control your emotions and feelings. It also becomes more difficult for those around you to decipher what you are feeling because you simply seem calm and relaxed. 7. Speak in a balanced tone

This is very important. If you want to stumble upon something different compared to how you currently feel, you may want to take a moment to think about what you are going to say and speak in a balanced, even tone to those around you. The tone of your voice can reveal your thoughts faster than you might think. Talking too fast or changing pitch very quickly and frequently is an obvious sign that you aren't quite sure what you are trying to emote or what you are feeling. Try slowing down before answering any questions. Other than that, try to speak to your mind in a logical context. You will need to focus solely on the facts and remove any emotion from the situation. By focusing on the facts, you can prevent your body from feeling the above emotions exclusively and focus on the task at hand.

If you can detach yourself from a situation you are in, it will be much easier to control your body language and the emotions you were putting off. An easy way to do this is to think of happy thoughts as good memories. Doing this will help take your mind off everything that is happening around you and make it harder for others to read your thoughts. By detaching yourself from the situation around you, you will more easily be able to see the logical side of what is happening and able to accurately portray the particular body language and emotions you wish to exude.

9. Talk to yourself

You will be able to tell your mind to think the way it should. This will make it easier to control your body language and emotions, as you are in the process of controlling your mind.

Conclusion

Overall, the reader is carefully introduced to aspects of behavioral psychology to understand why human behavior is complex and what motivates human behavior. For example, with the investment model, you try to maximize returns by taking certain actions. While the book invokes reliable psychological theories and concepts to make the content quality and applicable, the author ensures that the book is easy to read for any reader. Throughout the book, the author uses simple, easy-to-understand English with the understanding that the book's audience is likely to be native and non-native speakers of the English language.

Furthermore, the author systematically presented contents and concepts allowing the reader to build familiarity and complexity towards the end. The author presented the book as a manual, a guide and an informative piece on ways to read human body language. All of this was made possible through extensive reading of related topics on the subject from reputable scientific journals and presenting it in readable, easily recognizable and plain language. In this context, this book has succeeded in introducing the psychology of human behavior, discussing the role of analyzing people, ways to become a people analyst, and presenting different forms of non-verbal communication. Towards the end, the book discussed ways of mirroring body language, mind control, manipulation and ways to detect lies and deceit. As such,

Lightning Source UK Ltd.
Milton Keynes UK
UKHW032106030521
383075UK00005B/576